# From the Roof

*How the Haitian people taught two doctors lessons in resilience, love, and mercy in the aftermath of the Earthquake of 2010*

Doug Harty

CROSSLINK
PUBLISHING

From the Roof

CrossLink Publishing
www.crosslink.org

Printed in the United States of America. All rights reserved under International Copyright law.

ISBN 978-0-9826215-5-4

To Deb – I love you.  When one vows "for better, or for worse… in sickness and in health," no one really thinks they will have to live it.  She did, she does . . .

And, to all of the patients who I didn't see, couldn't see, wouldn't see . . . forgive me.

# Foreword

**"I**'m thinking we gotta get down there. How about you?" This was the first conversation Bill and I had after the earthquake that struck Haiti on January 12, 2010. We simply had to get there. These were our people, people with whom we had significant relationships, and in many ways, we had grown up together over the last 20 years. Bill and I, along with other doctors, nurses, and non-medical volunteers, have been going to Grand Goave, Haiti, for over 20 years to treat those in need of medical, dental, and spiritual healing (but actually, we have been the ones healed). We work out of a clinic run by Lifeline Christian Mission that is more than adequate. To be honest, on a good day Haiti is not in the best of shape, but after an earthquake of this size, we knew the suffering would be immense and profound. We had to get there.

I have been a cosmetic and family dentist in Greenwood, Indiana, on the south side of Indianapolis, for 23 years, and in that time I have been on over 60 short-term mission trips all over the world.

William Rutherford, MD, is an assistant professor of Clinical Emergency Medicine at the Indiana University School of Medicine and Medical Director of IU Hospital's Emergency Department, at Indiana University Medical Center in Indianapolis, Indiana. He was a Navy corpsman during the Vietnam era. He was heavily involved in air medical services for 25 years. Bill is truly a MacGyver and can make anything work. He is also one of my closest friends as we have been through a lot together. We have been together through some of the toughest days of our lives.

I have worked with Bill in all kinds of conditions in Haiti, and we know one another's thoughts almost without speaking. I hate to say this, but I size many people up by judging if I could travel with them, and I would go anywhere, anytime with this guy.

Lifeline Christian Missions has been in Grand Goave since 1980. Besides the medical/dental clinic, they provide school for 1,500 children in Haiti alone, and support churches and the spiritual growth of the people in various places around Haiti, Honduras, El Salvador, and Cuba.

This book is a compilation of the emails I sent during the two weeks Bill and I were in Haiti, from January 14-31. I started writing emails while on mission trips years ago as a way to communicate with my wife, family, and friends to let them know how and what I was doing. More than that, I wrote to get "it" out of me. The "it" was the sum of the pent-up emotions of what I was experiencing, feeling, and seeing. If I had no way of releasing all that was inside of me, welling up, wanting to explode, "it" would eat me up. On several occasions, when I was without the ability to email, I would get to a point where I could not sleep, or I would wake myself up crying.

This time, writing those emails helped me verbalize my experiences to a group of about 110 people. Because of the nature and tragedy of this disaster, many of those 110 forwarded the emails to other family and friends who might be interested. They, in turn, sent them to others. I honestly cannot tell you how many emails I received while I was in Haiti that started with, "You don't know me, but . . . ." They came from Afghanistan, India, China, South America, and from friends of friends of friends all over the place. It was more than a bit humbling to know that people even vaguely found my words worth the time to read. Many people had approached me suggesting that I write a book about my experiences, but it wasn't until I was approached by my friend, Joyce Long, who said she would help me in this endeavor, that I thought this was the time.

Here is how this works. These are my emails as they arrived to my friends on my "Trip List." They are raw, so to speak, in order to capture what was going on within me as I wrote. However, they have been edited to make them more readable. I am frequently writing while half asleep, making little or no sense. I have also added explanations to clarify what otherwise might be meaningless statements for those who haven't read my prior travel emails or don't have knowledge of my random, boneheaded references. Also, I beg for grace when the emails are poorly written or are amazingly stupid in places. Further, these are what I saw, what I felt, and what was going on around me. In several instances, I quote Bill without reference. We often talked through situations, to unload it emotionally, and to evaluate what we could do better the next time we ran across a situation. In the process, I reported it as my part of my own thoughts. This verges on dishonesty so I ask forgiveness, as well (but Bill says he doesn't care).

I could not have enjoyed this experience, learned as much, or worked as hard for so long without his friendship, love, and encouragement. Moreover, this is just a sampling of what happened during our stay in Grand Goave, Haiti. There are so many more things that occurred, so many more stories to tell, some of which I cannot talk about even as of this writing. I know I push the limits of what anyone can read at a setting as it is, so it is probably a good thing I kept my emails somewhat brief by my standards. Lastly, I rarely reread my emails. Frankly, I was a little surprised how much I wrote of our dependence on God. We were totally dependent on Him, it is true, but I had no idea that what was going on in my heart was coming out in my words. Anyway, here is my experience with Bill and my Haitian friends and patients, in Haiti after the earthquake of January 2010.

- Doug

# Table of Contents

# E

ntry #0 - January 13, 2010

**Hey to all!**

I have never written anything like this before, but I have been receiving many emails concerning the earthquake in Haiti. Carre Four, the epicenter, is the last of the suburbs on the way to Grand Goave out of Port-au-Prince. Grand Goave, our destination, is about 20 miles to the west of Carre Four, and that makes Grand Goave close to the worst of the devastation.

Bill Rutherford, an ER doc and one of my closest friends, and I are trying everything we can to get there ASAP. Bob Devoe runs Lifeline Christian Mission in Grand Goave along with his wife Gretchen. Gretchen is writing emails updating us from Grand Goave. Bob, like us, is also trying to get there from Ohio. It is tragic, and we are praying for a way to get in and help our Haitian friends. I am asking you to pray for the Haitian people, their government and for those already helping there. Please pray for something to break so that Bill and I can sneak in. The group I go with every year from the Indianapolis area is already scheduled to go in two weeks, but at this point it seems doubtful our group will be able to get in as the airport is already shut down.

Gretchen has sent emails from the Lifeline compound. There is a team of 58 women helping the women and children of the area when the earthquake struck. Lifeline is trying to get them out, as there are a couple of injuries. Also the second email was rather graphic in describing the injuries that she had seen. One was a little boy that had a traumatic amputation of his arm from the earthquake, and all Gretchen could do was wrap duct tape over some gauze as a pressure bandage. The other was a little boy who died during the earthquake. There is a lot going on down there and a lot Bill and I could be doing if we can just get there.

Thank you for your concern and for your prayers!

-   Doug

# Where to Start, Where to Start

**E**ntry #1 - January 15, 2010

**Hello everybody!**

I write you from a hotel somewhere near the airport in Santa Domingo, Dominican Republic. I am Doug Harty, a cosmetic and family practice dentist, and I am with Bill Rutherford, M.D., Director of Emergency Medicine at Indiana University Medical Center, and we were just sort of dropped by the side of the road. We were dropped on the side of the road while on our way to the Dominican Republic-Haiti border with a group that had mercy on us. They were giving us a ride to get into Haiti. We were going to the border because Bill and I had to get to Grand Goave, Haiti where the two of us have been going for over 20 years. Since the earthquake, we have been on a quest to get to our friends there. We were on the road in the bus and called Lifeline in Ohio to tell them of our arrangements and were told to get off the bus because we had a ride on a helicopter. But enough games, I will tell you of our fairly entertaining, emotionally up and down, six-different-plans day we have had today.

We started by driving to Tampa, Florida to catch our plane to Port au Prince. We were cleared for take-off, but not for landing in Port au Prince, so we had to hold for an hour and a half. As time dragged on, the pilots called them again, and we were still in a hold. He then talked to us, and it was decided to change plans and go to the Dominican Republic instead. On our way the pilot would call the tower in Port au Prince (run by the USAF) and see if we could pop in and drop us off at the Port au Prince Airport and get out.

Our plane was actually a private jet owned by The Outback Steakhouse Corp. The fee for this flight? Not a cent. They totally donated everything. Please remember Outback when you go out for dinner next time. And oh, it was so, so sweet! Nicer than that: Bill, I, Kim (an extra passenger), the pilot and co-pilot were the only ones on the aircraft. It is the way to go. During our wait, Bill rented two satellite phones, and they threw in a personal satellite locator, as well (Both of our families feel better tonight knowing this). If we get into trouble or need help, we hit the button, and they know exactly where we are located and precisely where to send help.

**The Journey**

When we finally boarded the plane, we took off with relief and wonder. Sadly we were enclosed by clouds. I nervously prayed, rung my hands, and rocked back and forth, hoping that the coastline of beautiful Haiti would greet us as we descended through the clouds into Port au Prince. Unfortunately, we ended up in the Dominican Republic. When they let us off, the pilots pulled out case upon case of water, bag upon bag of granola bars, etc. I'm not sure they understood how much that meant to us. I was impressed with their complete generosity. They were so happy to help us get into Haiti and equally disappointed as us not to be able to get us in, but they did get us closer.

Then things got really interesting. We went out of the airport and the security guy we were riding with hailed a cab. As we pulled to a stop, a woman in scrubs ran up, looked for and found her purse that was in the car we were riding in. I jumped out and chased her down to see if they are "going in." They were and invited us to go with them. We were so excited that everything seemed to be falling into place!

At the same time another group was "coming out" (of Haiti, that is) and heard us talking excitedly, and they looked at us like we were nuts. They really looked shell-shocked. A woman begged us to eat as much as we could because, she said, "You will not want to eat once you go in there!" This poor woman was wild-eyed. We are aware and prepared for this. Well, I know Bill is, and I think I am, but I also understand this is an "experiential thing" and may not be ready for what I am about to see at all.

Anyway, they took us along, and we had a blast for the first ten minutes. I decided I had better call Lifeline Christian Mission to let them know our whereabouts and eventually talked to Bob Devoe, who started Lifeline Christian Mission. Apparently there is a helicopter that is supposed to come and pick us up and then take us to Grand Goave. That would be hugely cool. It is going to take the women out as well. And that is why we had the group drop us off on the side of the road in front of our hotel, which is currently playing the worst karaoke I have ever heard. It should be good to go to sleep to. So there you have it. That is our status.

## Our Possible Plans

1. Go to the airport and get a ride to Grand Goave. It cannot take more than an hour and a half.
2. Get a ride to the border and then onto Port au Prince, then hitch a ride to Grand Goave, taking 10-12 hours.
3. Rent a car and go the whole way ourselves in caravan. Bill made contact with a group that are going in that way and said we could tag along. The people we are going with will return it.
4. The pilot and co-pilot of the Outback Air jet made it quite clear they will come get us if this does not work out, and try again to get to Port au Prince.

## Our Mood

We are good. We are guardedly optimistic. It is great that it is just Bill and me. We are easy with changes. No drama, just decide and go with it. And we generally know what each of us is thinking by just a sideway glance at each other as plans develop (and, so far, fall apart). Funny thing Bill and I have been talking about – People seem to think this is something great we are doing. Bill and I offer, humbly, this is exactly what we want to be doing. And more precisely, as Bill just said, "Why wouldn't we want to do it?"

Yet, we are frustrated because we know how many people need help, we could treat, we could pray with and comfort, and perhaps save from infection, disease, pain. . . it is killing us. Plenty of "we" in that last sentence. And "we" can do nothing. It is and always will be about what "He can do through us." We are praying so hard for God to get us there so He can go to work. I know you are, too, and we are incredibly appreciative. We both know how difficult this is going to be. I want to believe He is tempering us in reliance on Him, humility in front of Him, waiting on His plan. Yes, I am confused, but on my knees asking to be obedient in my confusion. I know we are closer than last night. We are closer to Haiti, to Grand Goave, and tonight, I feel closer to God. Thank you for your prayers, for your love.

[Lord, you know our hearts, our impatience to get to our friends and serve them by serving you. Help us to do your will, to understand what is important to you, to see your plan unfold in your way, your time, not ours. But if it matters at all to you, we humbly want to get to our friends, like yesterday.]

Cautiously optimistic ;) - Doug

# The Smell of Death

**E**ntry #2 - January 17, 2010

It is the smell unlike any other. It is the smell of death, of the dead. And in Port-au-Prince there is no escaping it. There are areas where it is terrible and some not so bad, but it penetrates you, fills you, envelopes you with its oily acrid smell. One area looked like it had been carpet-bombed, and the odor was so strong you could taste it and had to spit to get it out. The damage is fairly incredible. Yet, other places look fine.

I write to you from my favorite place in Haiti, the roof of our dorm. It is 10:30pm. The stars shine an intense brilliance here like nowhere else I have traveled, and it is a beautiful 75 degrees. We just finished clinics but more on that a little later. The sounds are not of donkeys braying, or dogs barking or roosters crowing. The sound is of hundreds of people camped out in the field. With their houses de-stroyed or too afraid to go in their houses, they came here where there are no buildings to fall on them, and they are just lying there tonight, as they have every night since the earthquake. I would guess 1,500 people. It is very strange as this field is always empty, but now is packed with people scattered on blankets or cardboard. Think of your favorite 4th of July fireworks and how people lay claim to their area by laying out a blanket, one next to the other, and packed that tightly, too. In the distance I can hear the moans of the injured in our clinic, or maybe I just think I can, but my ears are filled with their songs of misery.

Grand Goave took quite a hit with many buildings destroyed. I saw many of my friends that I have been worried sick about. Francois, Gary, Ti Francois, Moses, Emmacula, and Pomrose, and others I was so happy to see. I found out that Ta is well, and had another baby, a boy. When many of the staff saw us, they about squeezed the life out of us in greetings.

**The Journey into Haiti**

When we got up this Saturday morning, we just went to the airport and tried to find a ride somewhere. This is an entire story by itself, but I will summarize. We ended up with this British Search and Rescue team. As we talked to them, there was clearly something afoot. Then we asked if they would take us with them, explaining it was personal for us. We had been coming for over 20 years, and we had to get there. We ended up at a military base and flew in on a Blackhawk helicopter. It was a blast, and I had the open window seat so I could take some great pictures. We landed at the US Embassy, and I went out to hire a tap-tap and got ripped off but had no choice. A tap-tap is a small pickup truck with benches put on the back and a top on it, painted up brightly and also has religious phrases on it. The phrases help keep it running, or so it has been explained to me. It is a bumpy ride, and when riding in the back, it is not uncommon to crack your head on the metal roof, or support bars on the side. I wondered whether I had a concussion on the way here when we hit an earthquake hole and I bounced up to a good smack on the head. I watched Bill get hammered as well.

We had to meander through Port au Prince because of the destruction, and I am glad we did. It was a great, but sad ride, yet we were thrilled to get here. We got in around 4pm, so this wasn't bad timing.

## The Clinic

As soon as we got here, we went up to our room in the dormitory, felt a tremor, and then went to Gretchen's to have a pow-wow with her. She is amazing, and I will write more about her another day (as I have fallen asleep at the computer twice now). The town's hospital has not collapsed but has a crack in the wall, and the Haitian docs won't work in it for fear of collapse. So, they were with us. I am Bill Rutherford's assistant, basically, but can cut or sew if need be. Call me Charlie, except he would much rather have you than me, Charlie [Charlie Linville is a Navy Corpsman and an EMT with the White River Township Fire Department in Greenwood, In. He has been on several trips with us. Bill has shown him how to do lots of things, and Charlie keeps the OR organized. On the other hand, I am organizationally challenged.]. We do miss you, and hope you can fly in to help us out when not at work with the Navy, here in Haiti. I am finding where everything is slowly but surely. The other good thing is I have been around Bill enough, like Charlie Linville, that I know what he is thinking, so I don't have to bug him with questions all the time, which keeps us focused.

Bill is pretty amazing at this stuff, and tonight was Civil War Field Hospital medicine. Our first patient was a girl who had an open break in her leg in two places below the knee. Her foot was so swollen that we unwrapped it, and then cleaned up the site. [Just had a huge tremor and the people in the field are going nuts. It is still going as I write.] We used cardboard and duct tape to immobilize it. We had a lady with crushed arms, but while she was trapped, she acquired a staph infection also. We had several other broken limbs. We had to reduce a femur (Bill pulled her leg while I held stabilized her pelvis), then we used cardboard and duct tape on her for a full leg cast. We have no orthopedic materials. Then there were two spinal injuries, one being a paraplegic, and a little girl with a tear in her vagina. There was this five or six-year old that had her skin peeled away on her right arm. It was a perfect anatomy lesson of her muscle attachment and I could even see her bone a little. I mean it was peeled down to the bone in one place.

An older woman had a fractured femur (thigh) that had to be reduced. I held her pelvis, and Bill pulled on her leg until it was reduced to the proper spot. By the way, the ankle he was pulling was on was fractured as well. We bent cardboard and wrapped it around on three sides and duct taped it to death.

A man who had his arms crushed, besides the obvious, is having kidney failure due to myoglobin released from the injury site. We are expecting more kidney failures as people are starting to come that are still being dug out.

One that captured our heart was this 16-year old. As Bill started to undo her dressing, a wave of something horrible penetrated our noses and about knocked us over (I was gagging, naturally). I had never smelled gangrene. But as soon as I got a whiff, I knew what it was. It was actually worse than the dead of Port-au-Prince.

When we finally removed the wrap, she had a compound fracture of her tibia. She needs to have her leg amputated, but that still might not save her. Bill was so tender with her, telling her mother the options. We were trying to get the military to take her and do the work, but they mostly do just the Americans at this point. But even if that does work, she has just a slightly better chance anyway. If she heads south during the night, we will do it, without anything to make her sleep.

We will block the nerve behind her knee, to numb her really well, but will have to just hold her down. We would use a tourniquet to reduce blood loss, but we are without the cautery unit and will have to tie off all of the blood vessels by hand. It will take a really long time. The shock of that may kill her, the surgery may kill her, but she will certainly die if we do nothing. I have done this once before on another trip, but it was just a finger. When I run a fever, I can still hear his screams. This girl's mother just kept saying, "It is in God's hands."

That is how stoic these people are. They trust us, but wisely trust God more. We prayed hard about this, and as we looked through the bags again, Bill found some Propafol. So we can sedate her if needed. God is good.

It is now Sunday morning and beautiful out. The sun is bright as it comes up over the mountains to our east. The yard, several acres, is filled with people now, rising and folding their blankets, plastic, woven mats and whatever else they have remaining of their worldly possessions. The sun is warm and rejuvenates me, recharging my internal battery and giving me energy. And even from the rooftop, I can see that we are going to be busy as I watch people carry their loved ones toward the clinic.

We have more patients now that word is out that we are here. People are still being dug out and are being brought in from the country. We are the only game in town, so that will make us busier as well. We need supplies, especially Propofol (for sedation) and Rocephin (a strong antibiotic). An ER doc from St. Francis Hospital might be coming down soon, and he can bring it in for us. The Clarian staff may have something going on, so Bill and I will sync with them to make sure we are on the same page. We are a bit frantic today with patients, etc, and have not had an opportunity to communicate to that degree with the group back home as to our needs.

Church is going on, and the worship is outstanding. I am speaking to Indian Creek Christian Church, my home church, via satellite phone, but reception is iffy at best. The Haitians are saying that even the satellites shun them. We have had a couple of Navy choppers circling, because there are still Americans trying to get out from a few mission locations.

Bill and I agree that this is the place we are supposed to be in this moment. Our spirits are hugely great; we are satisfied, and we are trying to make a dent in things while serving our God. Pray for our patients--for their broken hearts and bones. Pray for those still looking for loved ones. Pray for those who have lost everything. We need so many prayers for strength, for wisdom, discernment, for health, for knowing when to quit. We are having a blast and working hard, but it doesn't feel like hard work. Instead it feels like joy. I am so grateful to be here in Haiti.

More later -- Doug

# I am Haitian

**E**ntry #3 - January 18, 2010

Anne Rose! Anne Rose!" Denny Claude called out as we followed him through the tent city that had sprung up over the compound tonight. This morning, I had slowly walked her 'home', which consisted of a few things that morning. Everything her family possessed would fit in a trunk. After Bill had checked out her knee that had a laceration and had been sutured decently, and he found she had cracked ribs we walked towards her ten-foot square that her family had squatted on. She had a crutch and held onto me. Several fine looking Haitian men wanted to help, but she wanted me to walk her there.

Tonight, in the dark, about 8:30pm, one cannot tell where she resided. But finally we heard her sweet voice. She asked us to sit with her. It was the highlight of the day for me to sit with her and her family and look out over the hundreds of people that are there bundled up because it is freezing at 70 degrees. There are little cooking fires and candles put in white five gallon buckets that announce they are selling food or drinks. And the stars are so beautiful as they blanket the masses. It was a moment of feeling what it is like to be like them, to be them, I am Haitian.

Bill asked if she had eaten, and I was struck by my guilt of not bringing her something. Her family has just had everything they own wiped out. She cannot go out to get something to eat because she is injured. She hugs and kisses both of us, and we get up to go, but I want to sit down and feel the energy of the crowd, trying to stay warm, getting ready for bed for the fifth night under the stars. Have I mentioned I love this place?

I don't have the words to describe the day we have had, but I am going to use every one I can think of until I do. Bill and I are in Gretchen's apartment at computers writing away, with Madame Bob— as she is known to the Haitians—asleep in her chair. I have cherry pull Twizzlers to munch on, and we are bone-tired, and yet I am so jacked I can hardly sit long enough to type.

## Clinic

It was about the only thing Bill and I did today. It was fast moving, spaced with periods of slow tedious work. I was obviously writing a little this morning and didn't get a chance to talk at church back home except for a few moments at first service. The satellite phones are useless. We had a number of tremors today, but not as bad as the one in the middle of last night. Just now had another rumble through.

I assisted Bill on I think three femurs that needed to be reduced, several tibia/ fibula reductions, and arms, fingers, crushes, and George's son's ear infection. Gary's wife had ketosis (she is diabetic) and Bill set her up with IV's and she was much better. It was good to see Gary. And for you Diane Braun, I saw Jean Rudy's mom, and she

28

said they are all good. She knew you would be worried and wanted to look for me at church, which is now in the area between the dorm and the clinic.

Francois saw Bill for the first time, and it was a beautiful reunion. Francois is our trusted driver and a friend that we have known for years. Francois possesses a laugh that is so joy-filled it is impossible not to laugh along with him. We have spent hours talking on our many rides in and out of Port au Prince, and while here after clinic. I had seen him earlier and he was pleased, but not surprised to see Bill and I. He said he knew he knew we would come, and he knew it would be the two of us.

Weadman showed up today and was a wonderful addition. He is a Haitian that was schooled here at Lifeline Christian Schools. Dave Pound sponsored him through Medical School, and he is in residency in the Dominican Republic. He is great to be around, and he also told me he knew and had heard we would be here.

I should probably explain that a "reduction" is when the broken bone that is not in the right spot is "pulled back" into place. You can feel it is off too, and it is supremely painful. However, this is Haiti, and the toughest people in the world live here. So, I stabilize the pelvis, and Bill pulls the leg until it comes back into alignment, and sometimes it pops, which is always fun. Now, the people winch but very rarely complain about it. I am pretty sure you could do a liver transplant on a Haitian without anesthesia, and he might turn his head slightly to express his discomfort. I'm telling you this is major pain. A lot of these need reducing because they were traumatically induced.

There was an 18-month-old whose left hand had a deep cut from the middle of the hand under the little finger to just beneath the next to the last finger. (Once I get my picture part of email fixed I will send it). The mom wanted it sewn back up, but this baby will never use it as the tendons are severed. [Another tremor.] The baby was quite cute, and it ended up looking better than what I thought it would. Bill does really nice work.

There was a lady that had a cool looking splint on her right arm, bandages all over her left hand, and her left ankle wrapped up. The splint was wicked cool. It was wrapped in gauze, but underneath was a firm, fairly hard, even splint that looked like a cast and was a great fit. It turns out it is part of the palm tree trunk, and they relieve the palm tree of it—perfect for that kind of use. It is rounded and physiologically shaped perfect. But under that was blue jeans that had been cut, including the back pocket, and it was wrapped like we would use gauze wrappings. It was styling, and I would almost break my arm to be that cool. Basically, genius in using what was available. But under it, the arm had multiple fractures, and it had to be reduced as well.

To reduce it, Bill strapped it by putting netting-like material on her arm like a sleeve, electrical taped it to her wrist, turned it inside out and then plastic tied the end of the netting to the overhead light post so that her arm was just hanging by her wrist. As she relaxed, gravity kind of got in the general area, and Bill pulled and squeezed it the rest of the way into place. He cast it with real plaster. I was trying to take the bandages off her fingers on the left hand. She was not having fun with my pulling and cutting the gauze off. I ended up using peroxide on it and then removing the tons of gauze. It turns out the finger wasn't set properly either. Bill fixed her left ankle.

When Weadman and I went to have supper, Bill discovered that she had a broken shoulder as well. So, she has a sling on her left arm for the broken shoulder, one on her right arm, and a broken ankle. Then she asks if she can feed her baby (as in breast feeding). We thought, sure, if you can find your breasts under all of that stuff -- I mean, she only has one limb undamaged. Here is the thing ... Bill is awesome, because no one had treated or even knew she had a broken shoulder, but he looks over everything because he says in these kinds of things you get so focused on one part and forget about the rest of the body.

We are collecting everything we find that might be useful for splints, etc. So far, we are saving paper towel rollers, palm ribs, plastic, and about anything we can find. We are running low on orthopedic stuff, but that is because we don't have any anyway. We hear there might be a team with another mission coming including an orthopod and a peds doctor. That would be great. Oh! Also a repre-sentative from Doctors Without Borders visited us, assessing problems and capabilities of surrounding areas while trying to figure out what others had and what we need. That will be good to know what is out there.

**Prayer Requests**

1. We need to find Bill's remaining two tubs. They have all of his surgical supplies, and we are going to have a lot more surgeries to come. Pray that we see it, can find it, that it glows, or something. We really need to find it.
2. The girl with the amputation went to Port au Prince. Bill gave the family money to get her there. And she actually looked better today. Your prayers helped her out.
3. We know we are going to see more kidney failures because of the number of crush injuries out there. Pray for those poor people that they can survive the three weeks for her kidneys to start up again (a little bit overstated).
4. Pray for our backs and knees. We are spending a lot of time on the floor treating people.

More tomorrow . . . we are having a great time, as we help these poor people,

- Doug

# Can We Come to Help You?

**E**ntry #3.5 - January 18, 2010

      Good morning to the world! It is 4:45am on Monday. I only write that to make it real for me. How can we have only been here since 4pm Saturday? It has been so intense that it feels I have lived a month in a day and a half, and I am satisfied and fulfilled beyond measure.

      The purpose of this email is to talk about the questions those you who are reading this have, and to clarify statements. I opened my email last night, and there were 65 in it. You have no idea of the effect that has on me--on my heart--to read your words. Do not hesitate to write. I read them all, but am unable to respond to any, so I am going to address some common themes here that people have been asking.

**Can we come to help you?**

      We would love to have anyone that wants to come, come. However, at this point, there is no way to get here. There is NO Diesel fuel, and no way to travel. The stations along the way we came were closed, and those that were open had lines that stretched forever—and were not places you wanted to be around. Tempers were looking short as we drove by those lines. God was with us when we got a tap-tap, the Haitian mass transit.

We know Haiti, are experienced travelers, and felt like we would get here one way or the other. We simply had to get here.

But in a week or two, that could change if they get diesel fuel that will allow more flow in and out of Port au Prince. Yes, we would take any medical people that could make it here safely. We just don't know how we would get you here should you come. Bob Devoe is still hung up in the Dominican Republic.

Bill says he would take ten doctors or two Navy corpsmen (that's how valuable Navy corpsmen are in our situation ... This coming from a former Navy corpsman). But we will take any doctor we can get at any time. The real hang-up is we have no nurses. It will sort itself out, and there is a team of Orthopod and Peds coming tomorrow to a mission here in town. If and when they get here, that will help gobs.

Hang tight! Those with medical skills would be great, and those with building skills are going to have their day for many days. So Leesa, I heard you and would love to work with you, and I know your husband's skills would be importantly used.

Further, we know about the destruction at Christianville (a nearby mission) and are trying to find out more of the situation each day. Today we will be even busier as it is getting out that two American doctors are here (actually a doc and a half, since I am an "almost real doc" for you, Lil).

[Had to be gone for a while and just returned... even in the most tragic of times, there is beauty and wonder. A woman is giving birth at the clinic and I went with Weadman to watch, document and help. It is her first, and although she really thinks it is coming, her contractions were seven minutes apart when I left]

**What can I do to help you?**

There is little that can be sent to us, or that we can receive. Here is what we need:

1. An airdrop of medical supplies. Bill does not have his surgical sets, and this could be a problem if we run into more suturing, or putting people together.
2. I think I will write Senators Bayh and Lugar to see if something could be done, if and when I have time. Gretchen is working with Senator Grassley's office, since there were women from there stuck here, and she had been in contact with them.
3. To be blunt, send money to Lifeline, or the organization of your choice. If you want to affect me personally, besides Lifeline, I work with, and am supported by CGI, CenterforGlobalImpact.org. They have given me money directly to buy supplies since I am on the board of directors.
4. Pray, pray a little more, then pray a bunch more …

## How are we doing?

I am completely aware these emails have kind of gone viral and am humbled by the thought of people actually getting meaning from them. I mostly write to keep those who love me up-to-date and for psychological balance. I need to get this stuff out of me.

Emotionally we are good. I have seen some hard things, but that is what I have fully expected. The 16-year-old with the leg was rough, but it is what it is and has really been okay. I really haven't cried yet, which is weird if you know me, but it is moving so fast and the situation is so fluid that I am good with it.

We do miss our wives. There are times I wish someone would just hold me for a moment and let me kind of melt and feel their love. I would just like to be held, and my wife holds me perfectly, the way I need to be held. TMI? Tough, this is what I am feeling. Further, we really thought these satellite phones would help us stay in contact better and are disappointed they are not. The lack of cell towers is such a bummer. Here is a phrase that captures how I am physically that a friend wrote recently. I am awake and aware. I feel so charged right now.

Physically we are good. Both of our backs are a little sore, and I would kill for a massage, but we have Advil so we are not suffering. It's a minor complaint when we are seeing what we are seeing. We are feeling well. I am taking my pills (for those of you new to the game, I had a liver transplant 13 years, 5 months and 2 days ago and have to take my medicines everyday). We are accountable to each other about it (for you Linda). But all is good.

We do a lot of our work sitting cross-legged on the floor working on those who are on mats, blankets, or what have you. Yesterday, I was cleaning the wounds of this high school kid and had him sit on my chair, and I sat on the floor and put his foot on my leg so I could clean and dress the areas that were skinned from him as the blocks fell all over him and his family. The Haitians had a fit that I gave him my chair and had his foot on me. But I ignored them and quietly began carefully cleaning, wiping and dressing each wound. I looked up at one point and saw his mom crying.

## Sleeping

Not much, but I haven't needed much. I wake up rested with the first huge tremor about 3 or 4 am. I am staying up late writing, but then on the roof where I pray for our patients that I can remember, for my family and friends that I know are reading this, and for those patients we can't see or haven't seen yet. Here is the killer: I am hardly drinking any coffee down here, like only four cups or so... that I am this alert is amazing to me

**Explanations**

When I say we are "having a blast," I mean that we are doing exactly what God wants us to be doing in this moment. Certainly, there is no disrespect meant as we are living in this tragedy of incredible proportions. I know I keep repeating this, but it is such an incredible feeling to know He is with me, us, in every moment. Totally can get into this… but when you are so focused on God, our patients, and you guys, all the distractions are gone. It is great! Are we having fun? Absolutely. Not in the classic sense, but when we are doing this kind of work really, really helping someone; it is fun. We are so humbled by the toughness of the people when it comes to how much they have lost and do not complain about their loss unless it is a loved one.

I thought we might be a little hungry since we knew food was a little scarce. We are eating well, like, too well.

I wish I had the words to express what is going on inside of me. I am so fulfilled, so satisfied, so passionate about the Haitians. Both Bill and I believe we HAVE to be here, and now that we are here we are thrilled.

We laugh a lot. There are lots of funny times throughout the day. Missed translations, things that occur to us that we should have brought and didn't, and things that are too out there to talk about, at least for now. What happens in Haiti, stays in Haiti, is our motto as we do things we would never do at home in our jobs, but you have to do what you have to do.

**Prayers**

1. For a drop of medical supplies.

2. It would really help if my Creole would come in, fluent, and I have been begging God for years to give me this tongue. Maybe I need more help in that, or maybe He laughs Himself sick watching me trying to communicate. Really I'm not too bad for medical stuff, but would love to be able to verbally comfort and find out more about people so I can pray with them better.

3. And today, I need to find that tub of medical supplies… it is here, it is hidden. Ask God to make it glow or something for me. Be sure and tell Him I am not all that bright and need a big blinking neon light or something to show me where it is.

4. For strength (and we have been markedly strong), for discernment, and for wisdom. We have our MacGyver groove going as both of us think out of the box well. But if He could just put a few more things in our path to discover that we can use, that would be groovy also.

5. For all the Haitian people who struggle on a good day, that they may find peace and comfort that only He provides.


It is time to shower, eat and then get on to it again. Thanks again for writing and for all that you are doing, and I can now safely say, all over the world, for us here in Grand Goave, Haiti.

Have had 2 really strong aftershocks that were impressive. Last night we saw people bringing in boxes of Ringers IV fluid. Bill came bouncing over to say he just found a box full of IV antibiotics. Yay!! We can now kill rocks or anything else that walks through the doors.

Bonjou,

Doug

# The Best We Can Do

**E**ntry #4 - January 18, 2010

"Dokte Doug, can you please help me push . . . ." Weadman requested rather calmly. And he was the only calm one. The woman that was delivering had quit pushing an hour before. The other Haitian women in there were slapping her arms, her legs, everything to make her push. Bill is at the business end trying to deliver this baby as best as he could. We pushed on her belly for around 20 minutes ourselves (I don't have an exact time as I was trying to avoid these slaps that were raining down around me like lightning strikes).

The baby finally came and took a couple of breaths, but not too convincing of ones. Bill had to do CPR to save this little one. And the baby eventually came around. To be honest, a fair number of healthy babies don't make it around here. This one starting out with this much trouble doesn't have much going its way. Bill doesn't think it will survive. This is why the custom is not to name your baby until it is clear it is going to live, or at least seems likely, like maybe the first year. I guess I can't blame them.

Not five minutes later I run into Ta, my assistant in the dental clinic, and care for her like she is my sister. She treats me just like my assistants do at my office. Well, but with tolerant acceptance of who I am and probably not going to change. She even gives me the same looks they do (and I love and have great respect for the women I work with, in case any are reading). I asked her about her family again. I tell her that she should have named her daughter Douglina. Ta tells me that Douglina had fallen and her front teeth were smashed upward.

She has me look at her, and Douglina agrees reluctantly (she is not crazy about the Blanc messing with her), but they looked good to me, and told her to wait to see what happens with them. She gave me that look like she wasn't sure about this. So I asked her, "Dr. Ta, ki es dentist, ici? (Who is the dentist, here?)" She smiles this cute little smile and looks at me. I ask about her new baby, a 1 month old, she tells me he is fine. I asked her if she named him Douglas, she grins with a gigantic grin and says, "Yes, hees name ees Dooglass!" I have rarely been more honored and proud. I wept.

We put casts on around 15 people today, until we ran out. Anymore, the casts are made of orthoglass, and are very light. The kind we placed were actual plaster casts . . . the ones you have to soak in water and then wrap around the limb, and holding the leg at an awkward angle, making sure not to bend it so that the fracture site that we had reduced by pulling (Bill at the ankle, me at the armpit) until we see it move into place or hear it pop (and I mean POP) and doesn't go back.

Using the plaster casts, anyone can take it off after 8 weeks, but with the orthoglass you have to have a cast saw to cut it off. These casts are heavy and tonight I can safely say my back is shot. A near fatal dose of self-administered Advil should help. We are casting femurs as high up as we can, and it is not the real way to do it, but the best we can do. A lot of "the best we can do" out there. Here are some of the stories:

[Really big aftershock – they come at night more frequently than the day. We hear them before we feel and see them.]

As I was walking around today in the clinic area looking for the baby whose hand Bill sewed up yesterday, I made eye contact with a woman on a cot who was in a lot of pain. I went over and asked her where it hurt and she was pointing to her side, above her hips to the upper third of her thighs. She had good pulse in her feet, and could feel me lightly touching them. She said she had eaten and drank today (they have been at the clinic since the earthquake and some have nothing, or have lost everything, and so they barely eat).

It did not dawn on me till today, and so I have been asking the question of food intake. How will they heal if they do not get nourishment? There are all kinds of philosophical discussions about patients depending on us if we feed them or give them money for food. So what??? The reason they are here is because they are dependent on our care. Besides that, I believe the Bible is rather clear on the subject. Further, how could I eat anything knowing she was out there starving.

Anyway, we are going to make sure they eat if we can help it. Moot point, cause she had. I promise her we will see her before the end of the day, even it is just before midnight, and I can see in her eyes how grateful she is. After we did who knows how many casts later, I had Bill take a look at her. She had a wall collapse on her and his diagnosis was she had a broken pelvis and it made perfect sense. So we took a sheet and bound it around her pelvis as tight as we could to stabilize it.

I went to get medication and came back to ask how we could pray for her and she said, "Pray for our friends who are still buried [they are dead], and for my body. But my mother is afraid all of the time now and needs prayers." I was holding her hand when I started, and she moved it up to her face and was rubbing it against her cheek. Then I felt her tears washing across the back of my hand, and when I had finished praying she kissed my hand and I was so humbled by the tenderness of her heart.

She had been in such pain for 6 days now and probably somewhere outside waiting each day to be the lucky one to come into the clinic for that long. And then to help her very little, and take a few extra moments to ask such a simple question, may have been the first time someone of authority asked her what they could do for her, as a person. As I left, I cried again.

There was an old man who was lying in the sun, and as I walked by I could smell it. This was one ugly foot with flies swarming around it. He was a diabetic, and his sugar was up, and being diabetic was why his foot is so infected in the first place anyway. He also has probably been sitting and waiting for 6 days. This guy will probably die, and it is because we couldn't get to him for 6 stinking days.

How many more are going to die because we couldn't see them in time. I'm not dwelling on this in my heart, because I know, and I think you have read enough of these to know we are working as hard and as long as we can. Are we sinning for not being quicker? I do not think we are. What else are we suppose to do? Bill and I talked this over for a couple of moments, but let it drop cause we both feel the same way, and what is the point . . . just have to let that stuff go.

Saw something I had not seen before today . . . a proviodine douche. This six or seven-year-old little girl had been hit by falling walls on both sides and she fell on broken glass had penetrated her and she had a vaginal tear. Bill and the Haitian docs thought he could see bowel inside of her. Also she had the beginnings of peritonitis.

There are a few times when you hear someone call out to Jesus (pronounced "Jay-zeus" in Creole). One of those times is when you are a 6-year-old girl, scared, in pain, and having someone probe you. I am here to tell you, and all who have seen him work will testify to it, there is not a more gentle, sensitive man when it is called for, than Bill. He was great with her, but it was one of those that are not much fun to be in the room with, and I am quite sure to have it done, let alone do it. I saw her later and asked how she was and she smiled and said "Bien! [good]"

I saw Adam today, and asked how he was. He told me he was fine. "Your fiancé?" I ask. He looks at me and his shoulders slump and he says, "We cannot find her." This almost certainly means she is buried in the ruble somewhere in P au P. I hugged him and told him I would tell everyone who knows him, and those who don't to pray for him and for her.

45

He knows she is already gone, and I feel so bad for him. There are countless more in exactly his situation, but he is my friend, and I really don't care about anyone else feels in this moment, I just know my friend is heartbroken. He is dying inside and I told him he was not alone in this and I wanted to pray with him later. My heart broke for him today.

Medecins Sans Frontieres came by again today, and they are so great. We talked for quite a while. They are going to set up shop in Leogone, closer to the epicenter, and more devastated. They said we could send our surgeries up there, and they are still surveying the situation in the surrounding areas. We told them our needs and they seem on top of it, so we will see how it goes.

A big shout-out to my second cousin (sounds like something they say in backwoods Ohio, doesn't it), Ryan, who was ordained yesterday. I am proud of you.

I went outside for a walk around, and it sounds so cool again. The stars are brilliant, I can hear singing in the distance of our tent city, and I love the sound the feel of it all, here. I feel so fortunate to be experiencing this, living in community with these beautiful people. Thanks again for supporting me in your prayers and thoughts. We are good and feel like we are accomplishing something important.

For once in our lives, here in Haiti, we actually might be saving people, and we pray not only from physical death, but more importantly, spiritual death. I am so fortunate to be here. I really can't still believe it.

**Go Colts!** (Did not even know what day it was—and football is so far out of my mind right now).

- Doug

# From the Roof

**E**ntry #4.5 - January 19, 2010

It is 3:30am on the roof and the stars are so bright, and exactly where they are supposed to be. I am content.

I cannot sleep and have finally taken the time to sit up here and just meditate, pray and breathe for a little while. The sounds around me are now familiar, like the old Haiti in many ways. The dogs are barking their circle around the city, roosters trying to crow the day in earlier, a donkey brays his complaint. The people below me and around me all sleep soundly, until the next rumble of an aftershock goes through . . . and we can hear the aftershocks coming.

I have been praying about what it is I am supposed to be learning. I was literally down on my belly asking for wisdom and guidance. This has been a spiritual walk like I have never had, and am trying to be obedient. I have never heard God speak, or anything like that, but not too long ago this thought popped into my head. If we had the surgical supplies, we would be overwhelmed in surgical cases.

I think I may have written about that yesterday, but did not understand the implications. I need to totally rely on Him. Although I have been relying on Him, I am still trying to control His thoughts, His actions. I am ashamed of myself for being so foolish. I guess I am a slow learner.

So today, I am letting go of the surgical supplies. We have exactly what we need in front of us and it will do. I trust the surgical sterile stuff will show up when we need it. We have enough Tylenol for pain management (yes, that and Advil is all we have for pain control, but you don't give crush injuries Advil … these people are tough and grateful for anything we give them).

We are dangerously low on Diesel fuel. It could be trouble. If our electricity goes out, we lose our Internet. Besides not being able to write emails to you, it is the only reliable way of communication to the outside world, the Navy, Lifeline Christian Mission. Cell phone service is coming on line, but intermittently. The Sat phones are useless. Also, I think our clean water will stop. This would be a bad thing as Lifeline has a spigot outside the wall that provides clean water the entire town. But God will provide.

Another tremor just now that lasted for a long time (whatever that is, and always seems long. Nevertheless, it was longer than most).

I am going back to bed, I feel like a burden has been lifted off of me . . . amazing what self-revelation will do for one's soul. Hope I dream of Haiti.

- Doug

# Loose Skin and Flies

**E**ntry #5 – January 19, 2010

I was pulling loose skin with one hand, and shooing flies away with the other. It smelled awful and I gagged just a few times. This poor woman, 37 years old, had awful bedsores on her backside from lying for 7 days. She had become a paraplegic the moment her world literally came down upon her during the earthquake. With bedsores already, she will not survive too long.

For about an hour I carefully, meticulously, as gently as I could pull that loose skin away. I knew she couldn't feel it, but I wanted to love her as best as I could, let her know someone cared for her and her family. I cleaned her up and redressed the wounds. The entire time, flies were so thick around me it was like a working in a fog of them. They are descending on those in the clinic like a plague and it doesn't bother the patients as much as it about makes me go ape over it.

By then my back was just about to cramp up after sitting on the floor cross legged for so long and I turned to look up to see her sister looking down at me with the sweetest smile. You know there are not many times in life where you can really make a difference in someone's life by showing a little kindness. I was humbled by the privilege of working on her bottom, and I never thought it is something I would say.

I bent down to ask my patient how we could pray for her and she was so quiet, or the clinic was so loud I had to get down on my knees with my ear next to her mouth. She asked me to pray for her family, that they would take care of her. She asked me if people like her could walk again in heaven. It took me a minute, with my face hanging down to get myself together, but I whispered into her ear, the translator's mouth next to mine. And we prayed that her family would love her, and care for her all of her days, that they would see the beauty of the woman before me, that her children would know how much she loved them, and that she would walk again. Then I promised her that everyone walks in heaven, and dances and sings all of the time. And she kind of laughed and grabbed my hand and said "Mesi, Dokte!'

That was the kind of day I had. It was perfect. First thing when I woke this morning was to tell Bill about the revelation about the letting go of the surgical supplies while praying on the roof last night. Said that I thought I had learned that lesson years ago and he just laughed and said, "You aren't the only one here with control issues." We are used to running the show, and if we don't we should be, so we think.

We got going at 7:30 and hit it going hard. There were 2 Colle's fractures. Those are where both bones of the arm have broken just above the wrist. Bill injected some lidocaine in the fracture area, and then just pulls on the wrist with one hand and the elbow with the other until the bones line up. The injection doesn't kill all of the pain, but enough to do it.

We found a bag of orthopedic stuff and dug out an arm braces for them. We gave her some Tylenol and prayed for her and sent her along. Most of the reductions just pull on it with no anesthetic or anything. They may wince but rarely verbalize. My job is usually to hold the pelvis in place, or pull up under the arms. Sometimes it pops. Didn't have more casting material so that didn't do any more.

Anne Rose's knee is now infected and that is worrisome. The cut she had must have been deep with some damage. It really hurts her, and she is not one to complain. There is an orthopod coming in 2 days (we will believe it when we see it), so hopefully we can get her some help. She is so great, and has helped us for years. They have lost everything so we give her money every day to make sure she can get food for her and her family.

I cleaned and dressed 2 more bottoms today. One lady has a broken pelvis, and she was hurting, especially when we rolled her on her side to clean the wounds. When the blocks fall on people it just kind of peels the skin off. So it took me a while with her moaning. I felt bad about it, but she was very happy when we got her bound up in a sheet so her pelvis was a little tighter.

Bill Rutherford just amazes me every time I work with him. We are both collecting anything that might look useful to use as a splint or something that might be molded into a medical devise of some sort.

Today we had come past the "devastation" mode and now are into the "crisis" mode. We are trying to clear out those who don't need to stay, and move those that are going to need surgery. We put all those patients on the south side where my dental office is. It looks like a Civil War hospital with beds on the front porch. There are 3 paraplegics, 3 feet that need amputation, and several other breaks that need attention, but will see what this orthopod thinks when he comes.

I am telling you it is well-organized. We can run over and give 2 Tylenol to every patient at the same time, change dressings all at once, and be organized and efficient. The church room is completely clear except for a couple of patients that are just living there for right now. One lady we went over to look at was very old and had cataracts, and a stroke. Her daughter was feeding her rice and beans and this little old lady was wolfing them down like she had never eaten before. We all stood in wonder as she inhaled spoon after spoon. There is something about watching someone really enjoy food that much, particularly because she didn't have a tooth in her mouth.

Tomorrow some of the Haitian docs are going to other villages to triage and send people our way. So we could get busy again, but we are really running low on material. Bill and I are quite calm about it. Doesn't matter anyway, we can do nothing, so we will work until we have nothing left and figure it out after that.

Also, we may have to amputate the foot of a guy that is gangrenous. It has "the smell," and in fact the people were having a fit he was with them in the ward as they thought breathing gangrenous fumes could make them get infections too. So to keep the peace, I asked the daughter if we could move him onto the other side, and promised he would be the first one taken care of by the orthopod.

Bill and I talked it through tonight, but we really don't want to take his foot. And the guy is really old and out of it. We will let the daughter decide. We can do it; we just don't want to do it. Bill is a gifted physician and jack of all trades and I know he can make it happen, but this guy is not going to make it. Pray for us on that issue.

I am so tired, so I am going to wind it up. Tonight at dinner, we talked about the emotional toll it is taking on us. Not really all that much, but we have all cried and I have almost every day. These people that have little to begin with and it is all gone. The heartbreak of Adam not being able to find his fiancé, let alone the vision of piled up dead bodies, and the smell of it all it Port au Prince, and Leogane, especially when you drive by a building that reeks and see baby clothes hanging out of the pancaked house, etc. And knowing that we could have saved some people that are going to die because we did not have the right materials, or enough of this, or worked quicker… But as Bill wrote in one of his emails, "There is no place I would rather be." And I will add, you could not keep me away from here. I love these people.

Thanks again for your prayers... they are working. We will run out of diesel tomorrow and that means no electricity for sure. Love to my fam . . . thank you.

- Doug

# Earthquake

**E**ntry #5.5 – January 20, 2010

Woke up to the alarm this morning. The Alarm. Apparently a 6.1 sort of alarm. We are all fine, so no worries. We are having aftershocks every few minutes but they are very mild. Funny because in Indiana, before this, these little aftershocks would have been talked about for days.

The other funny thing is when someone is fumbling with the doorknob to get out during a 6.1 tremor, how your mind works. I was thinking, almost amused, "So this is how people die in these ... someone cannot get the door open and the building collapses around you and you are buried."

Also, as I ran down the stairs, as always, a song of the day/week/month is pounding away in my skull. The song I can't get rid of right now is "Hey Ya" by OutKast, but this version is by Obadiah Parker and is mellow. As I was blasting out of there, I can remember in my head was going, "Heeeey, Yaaaa, heeey Yaa!" I think I need some serious treatment, sometime soon.

As soon as we got down stairs and realized the building was as sturdy as it gets, we immediately ran up to get pants for me, Bill grabbed his bag, and we took off running for the clinic. We ran over, looked quickly, assessing everyone for injuries. There were people with their hands up saying, "Mesi Jesus!" But all were fine. We then went out to the church to check on everyone, and they were all ok. "Mesi Jesus," from me as well.

We then went through the hundreds of people who are still on the property to see if we could see anyone that need help. We were doing this for everyone, but as for me, and I know Bill's heart, we were actually looking for Anne Rose, our Haitian Scrub Nurse with the bad knee injury. We saw her brilliant smile from 40 yards and she was waving at us. She knew we would come. We love her, and she us, and it was a relief to know she was well.

We will be waiting to see if this latest earthquake brings anyone else too us, and hopefully not amputating that poor man's foot, then Bill and I are going to the next little town over to see if we can help or send people our way.

We are starting to run low on duct tape as well. Sounds goofy, but you have no idea how useful that stuff is to us. For holding on bandages, to using for pressure bandages, to wraps for make do splints . . . and yet, neither one of us is particularly concerned about running out. There is nothing we can do about it, we know help is on the way, and I don't think I have written about that.

There is major political muscle moving on our behalf this morning. It would not surprise me to see helicopters flying over us with diesel or supplies at any moment. We have learned to be Haitian on these things, however. They are the most patient people I have ever been around, or with.

One last thing . . . Bill and I had a chance to sit on the roof last night and unpack a bunch of stuff, and just chat. It has been so intense that we have just dropped into bed. We have had no time to be together and relax. We laughed ourselves silly over who had the most bars on our phone so we could send texts and emails. I had all kinds of stuff but could not call. Bill moved his chair all around trying to catch whatever I had going on. We talked about things that needed outing, emotional stuff that we needed to talk about, and also how we had the best wives in the world to know us so well to allow us this. I think for the first time I realized how fortunate we are to be here when so many are trying to get in but can't.

After he left, I read some emails that you have been sending and had a major emotional release (read: cried like a baby). I could feel it building but had no outlet. We are trained to box that stuff up and deal with it later. Yes, I shed a few every day, but no way to un-package it. To read your emails of love and tenderness was just the turn on the spigot I needed. It felt good to let it out. I feel tremendous this morning, in spite of the rather odd wake up call.

The sun is on my face now, and there is nothing, nothing more beautiful than watching the sunrise over Haiti. In case I forget to tell you all, I love this place, these people. Thank you for your prayers and joining on this endeavor. We both feel the calmness and focus of people praying for us.

# View from the Roof

Good morning and have a great day.

From Haiti . . . Doug

# The Wailing

**E**ntry #6 – January 20, 2010

It's the wailing, the wailing, and the wailing that gets you in the pit of your stomach. The flailing of arms and flopping about, the sounds from the deepest part of their souls and you know by watching, hearing, and feeling their display that it is how you would feel, and feel it for them.

We lost someone in clinic today, thus, the wailing. I was walking around the tent city, just checking things out, experiencing the people when someone ran up to me and said a woman was having trouble breathing. I ran over and her breathing was labored at best, HR of 120, and burning up. I ran to get Bill who was taking a couple of minutes to get some lunch and we ran out. Right away he ordered her carried to our room. Bill was in his element and is amazing to watch. He started a line in her neck (external jugular) and we were pouring fluid in, and he was giving her antibiotics. I went to tell Gretchen what was going on over there, and when I was about 30 feet away from them I heard them and it stopped me dead in my tracks. I walked past them and saw Bill approaching me shaking his head, but I already knew.

It is not that people don't die, everyone dies, they just do not do it on our shift . . . and we take it personal. She was a femur fracture that we were going to send to Leogane to have surgery. She was the sweetest thing and always smiled and squeezed my hand when I would bend down and ask how she was. We did everything possible with all that we had. If she was dehydrated, or septic we might have been able to keep her if we knew sooner. Who knows what her real cause of death was, but Bill thought it was likely a pulmonary embolus, or clot to the lung. We are fine with it and doing well. I am doing well. Bill and I have talked it through. I choked, but didn't cry . . . most of my tears were already used up.

A 6 year old boy came in with a bandage over his head and right half of his face. I removed it until it was stuck to the wound near and around his right eye and cheek. I held his arms and legs as Bill poured on some peroxide on the bandage to loosen it free from the wound so it would hurt as little as possible. As Bill gently lifted it up, there was just a gouge where his eye and a portion of his cheek used to be.

I told myself to get cold, to separate, to be apart from it, but I could not and gently wept as he cleaned him up. I am not ashamed of crying; it was just too much, too close, too awful. I never lost control, but just had to keep my tears from dropping on the work area. After Bill turned away for a few seconds to gather himself, he dressed it and we prayed and sent them on their way. But that one will stay with me for a while.

We are now out of non-sterile gloves. We have tons of sterile gloves so we are ok, it's just another sign we are running low on everything. We talked and Bill said if we can have a roll of duct tape, a leatherman, and a zip tie and he can probably fix anything. From what we have been doing, I would say it is true.

**Good News!!!**

We saw the baby that was delivered the other day (a girl) and she looks really good. Has a seizure disorder, but has a strong suck. The mother says she doesn't have any milk, but we are sending over Matild to straighten her out. Matild, also known, as Sergeant Major, will make it happen.

The lady with the bedsores smiled at me today and when I asked how she was, she said she was much better. Certainly she is the same physically. We are trying to make contact so that they can go to the USS Comfort for help.

Finally got some cell service today. It was good to communicate with someone after the day we had. Bill and I took a walk around town this afternoon. We needed to get away, and I have not been out in since we got here. Saw some impressive destruction, and certainly can smell those trapped in the rubble. But it was good to get out and around.

The Big News . . . the team with the orthopod, pediatrician, and OB/GYN are here and came by today. Today of all days it was good to see some people that can fix up those who are suffering. They said there wasn't that much for them to do here since we have thinned out the herd. The orthopod is coming for a couple of hours to fix a few things and they are going to resupply us. But they have to see where they can be of the most help.

**Matt 5:4 Blessed are those who mourn, for they will be comforted.**

Tonight I mourn for the family of the sweet old woman; for the family of those we smelled and will never be the same; for those who cannot find their loved ones not knowing if they are dead or alive. I have been praying for them all day.

[Man, we just had another earthquake . . . this one was more sideways. It was rather strong.]

There is a rocking church service going on out there and I think I will wander over to it. Today I sat with a family in their tent in the field. I needed to feel in community for a while with these people I love so much. They started singing the Haitian worship songs, and it is like it should be . . . loud, sort of in tune, and with all of their hearts. I think they knew I needed it.

We are doing ok, really. I'm sure Bill is, and I am pretty sure I am. Our spirits are high, but we are exhausted. We have been putting in some big hours, and today was rather emotional. I am ok . . . I am ok . . . I think I am ok . . . I am broken.

- Doug

**E**ntry #7 – January 22, 2010
Hey . . . It is Friday night and this is from yesterday and I was not able to get this out . . . It has been so fluid today. Exciting, and fun and changing by the minute. I will write about tonight, tonight.

- Doug


Hey to everyone! We have had a great day today, almost all of it good, so you can relax. I apologize for the intensity of the last few novellas, but it is terribly intense here. That is what I love about it, but this time in particular has been over the top. I write to you from the dining area directly below the men's dorm room that Bill and I own. I am sitting in Patsy's spot with my feet up feeling rather content.

**"Whoever welcomes one of these little children, welcomes me; and whoever welcomes me, does not only welcome me but the one who sent me." Mark 9:37**

Jesus is talking about the humility of lowering one's self to serve others, brings you closer to God than almost anything else. So what about when the little children welcome you? Love you? What about while trying to serve, you are out-lowered? If that even makes sense. I will explain.

I left you last night broken and emotionally exhausted. That soon changed. After emailing you, I heard singing from the church service going on, went over and sat down. Before I could get settled I had a 4 year old boy and a 6 year old girl come over and sat on my lap and just looked up and smiled the biggest grins you can imagine.

They started playing with the hair on my arm, my face and hair, and as I tried to sing along to the Haitian worship songs they came unglued. I needed to be loved on a little, and they restored my soul. Two "little children" welcomed me back to Him. I also made some calls to people who keep me grounded and just needed to hear their voices. It felt great.

We had to say goodbye to Weadman today. He has to go back, but it was beautiful to see him come over here for his people. I love that guy. He has an 11-hour bus ride ahead of him, and it is hot out . . . poor guy.

I slept 4.5 hours last night (most so far) like a rock and was really rested this morning, which started off with a bang. We saw the kid with the eye and brought him into clinic, and we think we saw his eye in there, which is cool and made us feel lots better. As we were cleaning it out, I could see his skull and the wound that went up and under a bit towards the top of his head. We ended up getting him transported.

I started out today with having the privilege of changing the dressings on a woman that had a huge chunk of her leg removed. It was not hard work but very enjoyable to serve a woman that had nothing and then to pray with her. I did a spectacular job and it looked great, thanks to Janet for her wound care tips.

I talked to a woman that has breast cancer and wanted to know if she could have the chemo here instead of Port au Prince. No one carries it, we are told, and I know she is not going to PaP for treatment. So I gave her what I could, a prayer, a hug, and a few $$ to get her there.

OK, this is how the rest of our day went. About the time we got finished with the eye, there was a girl who had some holes in her scalp that needed sewing together, a girl with about a third of her forehead tissue scraped off that needed treatment, and then MSF, the French initials for Doctors Without Borders came by.

We had been expecting them and they have been incredible to work with, checking on us (I really think that they did not think we were up to the task, but we have been hearing from other groups "So you're the 2 guys from Indiana that have been doing . . . .) Anyway, Matthew came to make sure we were good to go for our patients and to see what we still needed. He didn't have anything, but when he did he would get it to us.

They leave and then another group from MSF shows up with a really nice bus to take our patients to Leogane for surgery. We have 2 amputations, 3 or 4 femurs that need surgery, the kid with the eye, the forehead, and a one who has crushed arms, etc.

I am trying to help the Haitian doc find all of them, and then the Marines show up. Yes the US Marines walked in looking for "the 2 docs from Indiana." We have used every person we know that had connections with Congress, the Senate, everything to get us food, diesel fuel, and medical supplies. They need to know what we need, and what we are seeing now (walking wounded, mostly), etc. We were their first stop when they landed on a road on Leogane. It was pretty cool to see them roll up. Well-organized bunch.

On top of that the Marine Environmental Officer comes walking in, and wants to know our needs and thoughts. We need latrines badly. What used to be people laying on mats and stuff on the grass has now turned into people bringing in wooden poles and plastic sheeting, palm fronds, etc and they are using the bathroom everywhere (ask me how I know). It has not rained yet hard, but when it does, that is how cholera, and dysentery get going. So we are on top of that.

Then an MSF environmental team comes in and wants to talk through things. I walked over to talk to Gretchen but she was involved in a food distribution that was going on simultaneously in several areas. All of this is happening within a 45-minute period and it is chaos but great.

Our last patient of the day was a woman that was 8.5 month pregnant and had a broken pelvis. We wrapped her in a sheet and sent her on her way. Bill had a house call (tent call) at 11:30 pm. So it begins . . . our outdoor clinic is up and going.

We met up with a new group of 4 docs and sat on the roof and talked to them for a while. They are going to be a good addition for us. I am falling asleep and it is 145am, so I better wind it up. I know this is poorly written and please have grace as I am so pooped I can hardly keep my eyes open

Love to you all,

Doug

# Raining Babies

**E**ntry #8 – January 23, 2010

"Dokte Doug! Dokte Doug! Do you want to make baby now?" He said with a heavy Haitian accent. I told him Debbie might object, but my humor was lost on him. Thirty seconds later he burst out laughing. He said, "Doctor Doug, sometimes you are funny . . . ." Reminding him I was always funny, he said, "No, just sometimes," and laughed more.

We just had our second baby today. The first one was still born, right off the bat this morning. Thankfully, I met a team at another mission, and they had come to GG because they heard that we needed help, and were sitting in Jacmal doing nothing. The Lord provides. But they have an OB/GYN, with her husband, an anesthesiologist who delivered it for the woman. She was not too upset that her baby was stillborn, at least not obviously upset, but that is the culture, incredibly resilient people. But we still mourn for them. Tonight a little girl was born. The grandmother took off her shirt and put it on the daughter, and they had little booties (did I just write "little booties"), like you wear, and put on her. The culture is so rich in this country, and the love within families is great. Birth is such an amazing event.

I am in my place of refuge, the spot that so many prayers have been prayed, so many laughs laughed and tears shed. I am on the roof and am half-dead but fully alive, aware, and pristinely satisfied. We have had a day that has been so fluid and changing, fun, had patience tested, emotions and anger high, calm and peace that I only experience on a mission trip, and I loved and have been loved today.

My mind is still racing, and I am absolutely living in the minute, and for the minute—mostly because each new minute today came with a new plan, new place to go, and different time to do it. For example, I called Deb today and as we talked for 10 minutes, our plans changed 4 times. We were going to Leogane, then to Ti Goave, then to another place and then back to just this side of Leogane.

The excitement of that kind of situation is so great, and fun, like going on an adventure. The church having a full force worship and they are singing "Alleluia, Alleluia," one of my favorite Haitian worship songs. I can't get "Lover (you don't treat me no good no more)" by Sonia Dada out of my head. All is right in the world.

MEMO: When one of your best friends on the field with you tosses you a pair of shorts and says, "Here, try these," and laughs … maybe the pair you are wearing is a little ripe. Out of respect for those around me, I wore Bill's shorts from sometime when short shorts were "in" for men. It was not pretty. I probably shouldn't write this, but for the visual, the only clean boxers I had were Jerry Garcia's, so at least I was in the same decade with the lower half. Any picture you may see of me I made sure my Jerry's were tucked up before it was taken—not the kind of thing you want on Facebook.

Some house cleaning is in order. First, we did indeed get some diesel, or it might be jet fuel that can be made diesel enough to run the generator. I don't know how or how much, but the US Navy, and Marines are using Grand Goave as a staging area, and in fact might use the field behind us as a Landing Zone. Actually, as we were trying to get out of town today, I had to show a Lt. around the clinics to let them see the lay off the land. Turns out he is a dentist and wants to get the dental clinic up and running. Oh yes!!!

Second, I could not send #7 the evening before, because we did not get in until 1130pm or so, with Bill's tent call, and I also had the grandson of Matild who looked PTSD, examined him and had a doc do it as well, gave him and ended up giving him and injection that "would help him sleep, and he would feel so much better in the morning," if you catch my drift. Didn't see him this morning. Laura, a doc from LaPorte and one of the 4 doc to come by last night and help us, was impressed. We are seeing a fair number of that sort of thing, and it is growing. But after the earthquake, how could it not?

Third, I could not send yesterday morning because we hit the road running at 7:30. The funny thing is we have to stop and think about what day it is. I don't think I have ever had to concentrate this much. Things are changing so quick that everything is being rethought all of the time. Particularly, when we were running out of supplies and looking around for anything to make a splint. We even reused those palm bark splints.

I can tell you one thing, I will never look at a paper towel tube again in the same way. I don't know how it works in my brain. The days fly, they run together, we can't remember whether it was this morning something happened because it seemed to be two days ago.

Also had the MSF showed up again to check on us, love those guys. This group of 4 docs had us a little worried. I was afraid there might not be anything going on that would make them feel they were valuable to us. To be honest, just having someone else here is valuable. And we needed them as it turned out.

Had the baby, as I wrote, but also had a couple of kids that needed sedating so their wounds could be cleaned out. As always, bandages had to be changed and I did this little old lady with a gouge on her foot. She kept pointing to where I needed to do it to her liking. Had a couple of fractures that needed a consult with the orthopod later, etc. The morning went fast and again had a fluidity that kept me hopping. Having them there enabled us to get out this afternoon.

We went to the other mission to get supplies and head out. We went to an orphanage and as Bill said, what would happen if you had an earthquake and no one showed up. No one was hurt or injured. Ti Goave (as in "Petit" Goave, meaning 'small bay') is particularly hard hit as well, and is a much bigger city. Just odd how things work, and so bizarre what you expect to see and don't . . . one town or area leveled and the next little area fine.

We ended up in a little tent city on the west side of Leogane. Leogane, if you have been watching TV, is about leveled, very badly destroyed and many, many dead. The people are scared to stay in their houses so they live here. No one has been there to see patients since the earthquake.

This is the kind of stuff Bill and I want to be doing—seeing the sickest, the ones that no one sees, chooses to see, or too much trouble to see. This is our calling. To say they were excited is rather understated. We saw a bunch of injuries, nothing huge, and probably 40 babies'.

The people were loud, crowding around, pushing, and surrounding each doc, and it was really cool. They are so desperate to be treated. I stood next to a lady cooking rice and beans over a charcoal fire as the sun was coming through her off white (whatever that color is called now), casting perfect lighting on us both. We talked, or attempted, and laughed and she let me taste her rice and beans and the other women were laughing at me when it about melted my teeth. But it was good.

Her kids were messing with me, playing with my ears, and they were so loveable. I looked around her little "house" of plastic sheets and palm fronds and she had a cooking bowl, an old plastic 2 liter bottle, a blanket that was as dirty as it could be, and a very few clothes. She had almost nothing, except she told me she was a Christian, and smiled the most joyful smile. Then she took my hand and prayed for me, as she saw me praying for others in line. I heard her say something about my family, and my children . . . then my sniffing muffled her other words. She then gave me another bite of rice and beans, smiling as she put the wooden spoon to my mouth.

# From the Roof

I love to watch the dynamics of a line in Haiti. They could not get any closer to each other if they were to be in each other's clothes. And because of that smashing into each other, it must look like a spastic snake from above. But we saw as many of these desperately poor people as we could. I really felt badly for them.

When we returned home, the group of 4 donated their supplies to us. We are so stoked that they gave their supplies. We will be able to treat so many patients with these perfectly timed supplies. God has blessed us with them today, and now they blessed us with those supplies. And they are legion. We spent an hour just organizing the pile. And then Bill spent another 2 hours afterwards. So our needs for medical supplies have dropped down the list, but money and food for the Haitians is still critical, and diesel will also be a major factor in the coming weeks.

When I went to supper, Doug Pogue, was in there eating. He has been able to stop by lifeline for a few weeks, and it is rich to have him here. He was the music minister at our first church and I have known each other for a long time. He is a former EMT and will work with Bill and me.

We sat up here in the roof for a while talking tonight, laughing, and enjoying our time together. He brought me goodies from my office staff they had put together. Haven't seen exactly what yet, but he gave me the baggy of chocolate that I know a couple of women will love to see. So to you at the office . . . you are amazing, and thanks for taking care of me and loving me so. You are the best.

We feel so privileged to be here working. I know many of you would love to be here. I don't usually feel we make a big difference physically, on these trips, but just spending time with people and listening to their stories of hardship and then praying for each patient is huge in its own right. But this time, I really feel we may have saved lives, I know we saved lives. But not because of anything we do or have done. It is because God wishes to heal each of these amazing people.

We pray because the humbleness of hearing someone share their hearts, and then ask the Lord to hear their/our pleas is one of the most important things anyone can ever do for each other. And we touch our patients constantly with a rub or a hand on them because people want to be touched, and held, and loved, and we recognize the healing power of touching another person. We are so fortunate to be here.

Our translators, Ben and Isaac, have been putting in every hour we have. I tried to tell Ben he could go home the last couple of days, but he would not. He told me that he could not think of going home if we were working. He told me no one had come but all of those that work at Lifeline knew that Dr Bill and Dr Doug would come.

I asked why he thought we would come, and he said, "because of the way you cleaned that woman's sores on her 'buttum' (how he said it), because of the way Dr Bill always apologizes before he fixes the bones for people. You pray with everyone, both of you."

And as I cried he put his arms on my shoulders and said, "Dr, Doug, I knew you would come because you love us."

From the roof, under His stars,

- Doug

**E**ntry #9 – January 24, 2010

"Ki es sa? (What is this)" I ask. "My friend." He says quietly. When you are lying on a foam mattress on the floor with a catheter, and your legs do not work, will never work (short of God's intervention), your friends become anyone you can get. His friend was the biggest, hairiest wolf spider I had ever seen, and he was about four inches from his face. They seem to enjoy one another's attention.

I have really come to enjoy and look forward to taking care of these paraplegics. They are so broken emotionally and physically, but not spiritually. As I turn them, sometimes they call out to Jesus in pain, but they seem to cheer up a little as I come with my little sack of gauze, betadyne, peroxide, tape, pickups, scissors and a little of Janet's Formula.

Bill and I realized that a lot of the pictures we have of each other are on the ground this year, but you have to go to where the patients are, and this year people are suffering and suffering on the dirt. Every day I bend down on my knees and put my head next to their ear or their face and pray with them. I realize this may not sound particularly humble, but I so enjoy being there alongside of them-- relieving them of dead skin and decaying spirits. It really brings me joy to do this, and I don't even gag anymore.

The flies like to see me coming, too, as it seems like they are swarming when I start. I have become fairly adept at working with one hand and swishing them away with the other. They really aren't that bad as the maggots eat away at only the dead stuff, but it bugs me, seems too humiliating.

Today as I finished with my second patient, I had four people talking to me who wanted me to do things for them. As I got up, I was distracted. Then I heard this horribly stricken young man tell his sister that I forgot to pray with him. He was right. My heart sank. Conniving quickly I went over, picked up a couple of Tylenol and came back and gave them to him. I was smiling as I turned around, and I wish you could have seen his face when he saw I was returning to him. I bent down and prayed with him. It crushed me that I forgot to pray for him, but I covered it up well and I don't think he could see it.

How many times have I walked past people, did not have the time, was distracted, or just didn't care? Maybe they weren't on the ground. Maybe they just needed a smile at the store or a kind touch on the arm. I am deeply ashamed for calling myself a follower of Christ when I behave so poorly. Here is the thing: He turns around and He comes for me, and He comes for me, and He comes for me...

On a different note, sometimes things get translated you don't intend to get translated. There was this old woman with this terrible foot wound I was dressing. The entire top of her foot was peeled back to where I could see muscle and some tendons. I muttered, "How can someone with such an awful wound have such perfect nails?" I thought I had said it to myself, and I think it was Isaac who said, "She says wants to look at something pretty when she looks down." They were pretty, too. She was one of the people evacuated by the US Navy yesterday.

OK, so the Navy and Marines came to help us today, which was a riot. Bill and Doug Pogue (Doug, the Lesser, according to Doug, the Lesser) took off with a former Marine and a former Special Forces guy and went around the area to check out people. So that left me in charge. They showed up and asked what they could do, so I said, "Whatever you want."

I supported the corpsmen and docs in what they were doing with finding our supplies and meds that they didn't have (and they have almost everything—after all, they are on ship to support the Marines during an amphibious assault). Bill referred eight babies back to us, so one of the corpsman took a look at each of them. You could tell the lieutenant (who was a doc) was a good teacher and wanted her people to learn. There was a Navy corpsman who did a cast which was beautiful. Then they dressed a bunch of new wounds that came in. They treated about 100 patients and ended up taking four back to the ship with them for treatment. It was great for me to just lay back and let them do their thing and kind of relax and answer questions.

They helped a lot of Haitians today. We love these Marines and sailors. They make me proud of our country. I was talking to the lieutenant who was in charge of security. His Marines just got back from Afghanistan but were redeployed after one month home. He said they were going to send them into Cite Soleil, a hot spot for violence in the suburbs of PaP on a good day. He was glad someone had enough sense to divert them here. After that much time in Afghanistan, anything looks like an "insurgent" to them. He said this is really nice for them and gets them "human" again.

Tonight we had a guy who had a bladder as big as a rump roast (like I know so much about rump roasts, but that picture popped into my head). It looked so painful. Bill tried to cath him, but according to Bill, he had a prostate the size of a grapefruit (the thought causes me pain). So he did a percutanious suprapubic tap of his bladder, which was pretty interesting. After he tapped it, I had to duct tape it to the catheter bag. Only problem with that is that duct tape and vinyl gloves don't do too well together. As a result, I popped my glove, snapping urine everywhere. Including my mouth (and it didn't taste like chicken). We asked the guy if he felt better and like John Wayne, he said, "OUI!" in a drawn out, low, relieved voice. That made me feel better, too.

The last patient was a little baby who was dehydrated, so we got her set up with some rehydration packs. We see lots of that all the time. Speaking of that, we are starting to monitor our fluid intake. Since we have been so busy, we have just forgotten to drink. I mentioned yesterday how fluid our environment and decision-making is here. It is still that way. That's really fun but requires enormous energy and concentration. We are healthy and feel energetic, but we need to keep up on fluids and food. I continue to be amazed at the stoic nature of these beautiful people. They are incredible.

Another 13-hour day and Bill and I have "hit the wall" so to speak. It is 10:30pm so we are going to bed. I know it is early, but we are shot. I forgot to mention we were awakened this morning by a large aftershock at 4:30am--one that had us running for the door. I don't know how strong it was, but I had earplugs in and could hear it coming as it rumbled toward us. There is nothing I have experienced as unique as the feeling of something bad coming like the grumbling of an earthquake.

Last thing . . . thanks again for writing to me, to us. After a tough day, it is good to hear from people, even those I have not met. That takes us away from here for a few minutes, which is restoring. There is no place I would rather be in this moment, but the intensity is hard to turn off sometimes.

Sunday morning . . . we slept seven hours last night without any medical emergencies or earthquakes waking us up. I feel like a million Goudes!!! (Local currency that was worth about 35 to $1, but who knows what it is worth now?)

- Doug

**E**ntry #10 – January 25, 2010

About the paralytic . . . His friends loved him so much that they climbed up on the roof, dug through it and lowered him in so that Jesus could heal him. And Jesus' response? He forgives him his sins because of the faith of his friends. Not for what he has done, but for what his friends have done for him. This blows me away every time I read it. "Since they could not get him to Jesus, due to the crowd, they made an opening in the roof above Jesus. After digging through it, they lowered the mat the paralyzed man was lying on. When Jesus saw *their* faith, he said to the paralytic, 'Son, your sins are forgiven.'" Mark 2:4,5.

I know I am pushing your patience with the paralytics, but I have learned so much from these three this week. As I was preparing for church today, I wondered about their worship and what they were thinking. So what if the paralytics lowered me down to have Jesus heal me? That is how I am feeling tonight. I have seen their faith, their courage, their happiness, and they continue to teach me about all three of those things. I went over to see them after church, which is a whole other story I may get to below. I was stoked about changing their bandages and spending time with them. But when I arrived, the Navy corpsmen had already done the work. I was disappointed but realized the opportunity before me. I write this humbly, so you know exactly what happened, and not to bring any praise to myself, but for their praise and His Glory.

So I went to each one and laid down beside them, asking them how they were, if they had their medicine, and if I could get them anything. It was still pretty crowded with people running around, etcetera, but I tell you in that moment, it was just us. I got one a cup of water and another some Tylenol. The guy with the spider friend (who was out, apparently) said he was OK. They were all amused I had chosen to lie down with them to talk and pray.

He asked me to pray for his family so that they can build a new house. Since he couldn't work anymore, he didn't know how they would. Another asked that I pray for their children, that they would grow up strong, and would I thank God for still being alive. She said her family had lost everything and had nothing, not even clothes to wear. Could I please pray for them to have enough? So I prayed for new houses, for mercy, for strength and protection of children, wives and husbands; for giving of life and for long, fruitful lives; for enough food, water, shelter, love; and for Jesus to come soon. Please come soon. Then I stood up, walked around the corner and as I held on to the wall weeping, I asked God to teach me to pray like that, to not ask for anything for myself.

It turns out, according to Francois, that Grand Goave is the new Port au Prince. It is growing. Before the earthquake there were 7,500 people here. Since the earthquake there are 11-12,000 people. Who can blame them? There is security here with lights on at night, and there are potentially jobs out here because of Lifeline. There are new tents set up all of the time and more patients.

Church was absolutely packed today. I have never seen it so crowded. And in spite of all of the death, destruction, and misery, these people are helpful, happy, and singing songs of thanks. They amaze me, and I am so blessed to see this. I tried to take a shortcut to clinic today and ran into a dead end of tents. But the families would not let me turn around. They pulled up the corner of their blankets and lifted up their plastic sheet walls and then yelled at the people behind them to do the same. So I cut through their apartment's living room walls of bright green, and blue, yellow, and patterned snowmen bed sheets, Teenage Mutant Ninja Turtles, and sunflowers. I tip toe around foam pads, blankets of every sort, and woven mats, of places that are family bathrooms, or places where someone finished squatting as I approached. I duck under wires, cord and plastic bag rope until I open up into the clinic. Every person has been pleasant and beautiful to me, if not entertained. I do not think I would be the same under the circumstances. They are joyful and thankful for what they have. At every church service, they sing their hearts out. Also I love to hear Haitians pray at church. Everyone prays out loud and at the same time. It is so cool to be a part of prayers like that. I always pray out loud with them and for them, too. It has to be like what God hears, only millions of others doing the same.

Bill and I lasted about 30 minutes of church. Then both of us went back to bed. We have been beat, and a two and half hour nap helped us gobs. In clinic tonight, the guy from last night whose bladder was drained by placing a catheter in above his pelvic bone is not doing too well. He is a little demented and cannot keep his IV in. People keep taking out his IV or other stuff. It is killing us to have to restart him all the time. Also we found out the little girl with the vaginal tear from falling on broken glass during the earthquake also had a broken pelvis. Yikes! But she is going to get better. She is on the USS Comfort.

There is this rat about the size of a cat that wanders about the roof. Anyway, I am up here barefoot, and he just ran across my feet. That doesn't bother me generally, but this creeped me out. I am getting out of here. Well, that is our Sunday. Now I will head out to check out Bill and our bladder guy. Hope your week goes well. I know ours is going to be terrific.

Night!
Doug

**E**ntry #11 – January 26, 2010

Hope you all are well. I am on the . . . you know where I am at 9pm on a Monday night if I am in Haiti. It is in the upper 70's, with a slight wind. I can hear children playing in the plastic and tarp city below me. Dogs are continuously barking, and at least for the moment, no crowing about, but there are the simple songs of crickets in the round. I have my shoes on tonight as well! That rat still kind of creeps me out. Josh Radin is bouncing around in my head, now, and constantly, singing, "These Photographs." Hey there!

I can see the light of a ship out in the ocean, one of ours that brings us such relief and comfort every day. Bill and I have grown to love the Navy corpsmen and docs who come here every day. They are so gentle with the Haitian patients and have transported four more today. They are amazing, and I am becoming friends with several of them.

I won't use their names because I am not sure of the protocol, but there is a Navy dentist whom I worked with today in the dental unit. He did an I &D of a horribly infected 3rd, and I did a couple of teeth on a five-year-old that had smashed her face yesterday. They were so loose I practically could use my fingers. It worked out great, as I hate 3rds, and he is not that crazy about kids (teeth, that is). There are also a couple of corpsmen that I am getting to know and are really fun to work with. Also there is a Navy doc who is awesome. She is the one I think I wrote about that works with Paul Farmer and PIH in the central highlands of Haiti. You can tell she loves the Haitians and gets what we are about. Bill and I have both commented on their professionalism, and like Bill and me, they love to teach as well. The Haitians talk about them, too. I am proud of them and of our country to get this involved in a place that many forget. Not only that, but they relieve so much misery, that it would take Bill hours to go through with his trusty assistants Doug, the Lesser (Pogue), Mary Beth, and myself (Doug, the doofus).

I enjoy having Doug P here as we go back so far, and he is a perfect addition and balance with Bill and me. He does anything requested of him with a complete servant's heart. He and I have been sitting on the roof a lot and talking. Bill has been off doing stuff in the clinic and checks on patients. He needs time to himself there. I know I have said I would go anywhere with him, but more so now. We really get along perfectly and understand each other totally, and more than that, love each other more than brothers.

**Updates**

Anne Rose is doing better. I changed her bandage tonight, but she is getting around better. I know the group that was supposed to come has been concerned about her. But she comes and helps the best she can along with that beautiful bright smile of hers.

I talked to Moies today, and he just came back from Port au Prince, where he did a funeral for someone I think was his brother-in-law. He is still quite sad, but he was telling me at least he had his body when so many did not. I asked how it went. He said it was OK, but with so many dead there, it was … and his voice trailed off. Moses is a wonderful man, and gifted translator.

**Patients**

My paralytics received regular beds today. Doug and I just went over to check on them. They are all doing great. I was away at the time, but when I came back, I wish you could have seen their faces. Their self worth to just be off the ground was impressive. Manfred, who was Spiderman for a day, was beaming when I saw him. When I ask him how he was, he always gives the thumbs up. Avril, the worst of them, was up emotionally tonight, too, but has been spiking a fever of 102.7. They have Foley catheters and can get infections rather easily. She now has an IV and is getting antibiotics. We are waiting for them to be transported to a Navy ship but have had other emergencies come up that had to go first. The guy with the suprapubic catheter was taken out today, and we are grateful.

We have a new worry, though. A little 12-year-old was smashed by falling walls. She was kind of crushed and looks really sick. She is sensitive over her spleen and liver. Bill could not get an IV in her, which about killed him. We gave her a gram of rocephin IM, and I can tell you from experience, that is not fun. But hopefully that will help her until she can be transported to receive better care.

Tonight, as every night, the crowd was worshipping God. The songs lifted up to Him inspire us yet humble us. These people are so poor, yet they are rich in knowing love—of each other, of us, and especially of God. I continue to learn everyday from them, from the sailors and Marines, and more than anyone, from God. I am trying to be open to Him, trying to serve and be obedient to His will, trying to serve the least, but they continue to out serve me. I am content and peaceful tonight. I realize how fortunate I am to be here, in this moment, praying and writing to you. I miss my family terribly but have His peace in knowing I am where I need to be. I'm out to the clinic one more time to make sure Bill is not still out there and also to say goodnight to my friends in beds tonight for the first time since the earthquake.

- Doug

**Tuesday Morning**

Last night after I signed off with you, I went back over to see what Bill was up to. It was 11pm and quiet. Anne Rose was with him, both organizing as best they can. We now have an abundance of supplies but will go through them rapidly with the surge in population that is taking place. He asked that I give Avril some antibiotics through her IV port over 15 minutes. He knows how much I am into these three.

There was just one light burning, casting a glow that was mellow. The ceiling fan's blade was hitting something with a soft "tap, tap, tap," as it whirled around. There was one cricket above the rest with his counter beat. The only other sounds were a low conversation between two men on the far end. I screwed in the syringe and just touched a little in, closed my eyes and breathed in deeply, slowly, and then slowly exhaled. It was God, our patients, and me, and I could not help but feel the wonder of the moment as I prayed for them, for my family (whom I am missing intensely), and thanking God for this moment, for all the moments He has given me. I am so content.

# Tired

**E**ntry #12 – January 27, 2010
I'm tired, really tired, so forgive me if none of this makes sense. We had a great day, bizarre, but great. We were awakened by an aftershock at around 5am. It was strong enough that we all rose up in bed. Then it passed, and we passed out for a while longer. Hey!

Our first patient was a woman having a baby. She was screaming. The women in there were screaming, and then Bill was screaming to get them to quit screaming. Doug Pogue was pushing on the mother's stomach, and Mary Beth was taking rather personal pictures. It would have been hysterical if we knew things were going to turn out so well. It was still rather amusing.

Bill was yelling that there were about ten too many people in Tammy's (the OB/GYN) room, and he's right--there were. This is a tiny room for a table, all kinds of supplies and 15 yelling, sweating people. I helped Bill reorganize the OR last night when we were really tired, and he asked this morning for a syringe bulb to suck the goop out of the baby's throat (maybe the grossest device I can think of, because Debbie use to suck the snot out of the kids, and it still makes me gag to think of it).

The problem, of course, is that I couldn't remember the reorganized location. He also wanted a clamp for the umbilical cord. I dogged-tailed my way back in to the OB room (now ten less people less but twice the volume, especially from the mother) to ask if he remembered where we put the clamps. He told me exactly where, and I got it to him in the nick of time as he was using that gross sucker thing. Yuck! The baby boy was now screaming, too. And then the Navy showed up with an OB and a pediatrician. They hopped right in. Great timing! We had three babies yesterday!

Then we had a boy who couldn't "pee pee," which is the universal phrase, wherever I have traveled. His bladder was the size of a small hog, and his mom said he had been that way since he was kicked playing soccer. The Navy pediatrician turned to me and said, "Is that possible?" I assured her that was not something boys of any age made up, especially since he had been cathetered once and didn't appear to relish the prospect of another.

In the room he said it was the soccer ball that hit him, and the pediatrician looked at me with eyes wide open. I told her maybe it was a cue ball instead, and she burst out laughing really inappropriately considering the circumstances. A Haitian American corpsman cathetered him this time, and it was not popular. It was at this point that I felt blood running down my neck from my eardrums that had finally ruptured from the birthing room screams, and now his ("rupture" is rather a poor choice of words under the circumstances). And it didn't work.

There was some discussion as to the possible cause and found myself about to scream, "The poor kid just wants to pee pee, for crying out loud!!!" The cath was pulled, and he tried to pee until I was sure blood vessels were bursting in his eyes. It was the funniest picture ever.

I was behind the boy, and there are six adult docs and corpsmen standing around eyes big, mouths agape, looking at this kid's "unit." You would have thought it was glowing or something the way they were concentrating. I wish I had a picture of the event. I had to leave for other pressing issues, so I don't know if their laser-like gazing burned a pathway up his urethra or what.

I just found out that last night, apparently, one of the paraplegics did not want to move to a bed. It was threatening rain, and we were worried about them getting wet. Anyway, Bill was trying to convince him, and he asked the guy if he trusted Bill. He hesitated. Bill asked him if he trusted God, and he said he did. Bill informed him that he was trained by God, and so he needed to get into the bed. And that is how all the paraplegics got a bed.

Yesterday the little girl with the tender spleen and liver area that we thought was crushed was not as tender this morning. We were trying to get her onto a ship to be treated. Ended up getting a hematocrit on her and it was 4.4, when normal down here is probably 12-ish. No wonder she was not real motivated to move. Blood was drawn and they were taking her on the ship to do some blood work. I feel bad for her and her mother.

Pushed antibiotics for 15 minutes for Avril, the paraplegic who is the worst, while her little eight-year-old daughter exercised Avril's legs. She was so cute and sweet so as not to hurt her mom. And she kept looking up at me while biting her lip in concentration.

While in clinic today, I had a translator come up to me and said this man had a problem I needed to look at. So I went over and asked the translator to ask him what the problem was. He asked him in perfect English, "So what is your problem?" And the patient says back in better English than I have ever spoken, "Well, my mouth hurts for days after I eat really hot [temperature] food . . . ." He was looking for some medicine that would stop that from happening. I told him there was a medicine, but it comes from God. He wanted to know all about this medicine. I told him it was called "common sense". The translator was rolling on the floor.

Doctors Without Borders came by and were giving out disaster kits today. They had a blanket and a box of something (cooking utensils, and other basics), tarps and other things. The place was near pandemonium, and it was right in front of where we exit the clinic. They were calling out names, and it was cool to see people getting something they could really use. So many incredibly poor people with less than the nothing, now have more than they had before the earth-quake.

We found out that Wittlynn, the Haitian doctor who has been helping us, is living on the street. I asked Bill how he knew, and he said he was compelled to ask. So he gave her $60, and I will give her more tomorrow. She is beautiful and smart, and we are really sold out on her. She asked if she could borrow some of our medicine today, and Bill told her it belonged to all the Haitians, and she smiled. See what kind of guy I am working with every day?

And finally, the last patient of the afternoon, well, it was 6pm, was a six-year-old girl who had a bandage that needed changing. She was wearing this white dress and was as cute as it gets. I could feel her sadness. As I pulled off the bandage, she had a four-inch gash in her little head, but it was healing in rather well. The bandage was stuck to her wound, so I had to get some peroxide to wet the bandage enough to keep from pulling. She did not flinch, did not move anything, not even her eyes, as I quickly yanked the last part free. I changed it and gave her a nice looking bandage that matched her pretty white dress.

When I asked how I could pray, she whispered, "I want my dad to come home." I looked up at her mom, and she gave me a quick shake sideways. He was dead from the earthquake, and I am guessing they could not find his body. I prayed for her, for her heart, for her dad to come home, for her mother, and her mother's heart. I said "amen", gave her a long hug, and she held onto me for a minute afterward. I bid them "Bon Soir" and almost made it to the corner of the building before I started to cry. I tried so hard to be quiet.

For those who are weary, He brings rest. For those who weak, He brings strength. For those who mourn, He brings peace. For those whose hearts are broken, He heals. And for little girls who have big gashes on their head and wear pretty white dresses and only want their fathers to come home, He brings … I don't know… I don't know… I don't know.. But as I finish this tonight, her whisper ringing in my head, as my computer screen becomes bleary and I sob too hard to type, I know this – That I will pray that He brings exactly what she needs as The One who sustains us, fills us, pulls up alongside of us, and loves us harder and better than one can imagine.

-   Doug

**E**ntry #12.5 – January 27, 2010

**Just a couple notes . . .**

When I went out after writing last night, I saw Avril, the paraplegic, who I had to give IV antibiotics. As I approached, she had 5 little kids lined up in front of her, perpendicular to her bed. She was moaning gently, and I took my shoes off, which made her smile, and gently tiptoed around her children to get to her left arm where the lock is located. I loaded it in a tiny bit at a time, and patted her, and she patted me back. I think we both needed it, as I was exhausted. Bill has been sleeping less than I.

Bill received an email from someone about a large orthopedic team that had flown into Port au Prince and set up at a hospital after their first hospital had operating theaters that were too badly damaged. We talked about it last night and both of us were incensed. After retiring to our bunks, unknown to each of us, we were both awakening periodically throughout the night about such a ridiculous email. I will quote Bill on this:

> *I read a posting tonight by a team that had just returned from Port au Prince. They were maximally frustrated because the blitzkrieg trip they'd planned was filled with unmet expectations and obstructions. The hospital they were expecting to work at was destroyed, the backup hospital had no water or electricity, the*

*anesthesia machines didn't work, their relief supplies were hijacked, they couldn't get resupplied, their "exit strategy" had to be changed, etc. By admitting their failure to plan adequately and exposing the flaws in the 'system' - the complete absence of a viable infrastructure, etc. they hope to help others avoid the same pitfalls. It is worth reading - but it demonstrates the difference between having laudable intentions, and having a relationship with people. One working definition of a disaster is to have one more patient than there are resources to handle. By that definition, Haiti is a mega-disaster on its BEST day. Veterans of Haiti know there is no reliable "system" -- ever. For a hospital in Haiti to be without power, to be so inadequately equipped as to as to defy the definition of "hospital", for equipment and supplies to be stolen by people who see an opportunity to survive one more night by selling their booty, to have crowds angry because they sense abandonment -- all this IS Haiti -- all the time. It's kind of like the scene from the original MASH movie where BJ and Trapper breeze into the hospital in Tokyo expecting to operate the way they would in the States and then catch a quick round of golf, only to find their plans thwarted by circumstances. One cannot impose one's will on Haiti. Though it is the second free nation in the Western hemisphere (the slaves revolted against their French masters just a few years after we raised the Stars and Stripes), it is also the poorest nation on this side of the globe. Haiti has never had a sustained period of political or economic stability. Fixing broken bones is important, but offering hope to broken hearts is even more important. When the Haitians see us cry because we have no medication to sedate them prior to reducing their fractures, they see that our anguish isn't due to our own inconvenience. They realize we are not just here to provide physical help--we are their friends. Expect nothing if you decide to come to Haiti. This isn't serving a single meal at a homeless shelter on a holiday while the local TV cameras role. It's a commitment from the heart. Planning is good and necessary, but the last time your plan will be working perfectly in Haiti is before you get on the plane to come here. Paul wrote that he had learned to be content with whatever he had, and such is required of anyone wishing to help here.*

My response? What he said . . .

Bill and I are not leaving until we get relief. Our patients need continued care, and more importantly, they need to know they are cared about and cared for. A team from St Francis Hospitals is coming tomorrow, we think. We will stay a day so that there is continuity in care and love, and then make our way back beginning Saturday, God willing. We are tired, and we long for our family, particularly our wonderful and loving wives, without whom this would be impossible. But this is where we belong, are supposed to be, and we love it, love it, love it.

# Full Moon and Babies

E ntry #13 – January 28, 2010

Hey to all!

Nearly a full moon to write by tonight. Just the rat and I up here on this roof, and it is nice to have some quiet, and a little stillness for a few moments. It is anything but quiet in the clinic currently. It is 930 and I told Bill I needed to cut out to write once we got things settled down over there. We were called over for our 3rd motorcycle accident of the day. He needed his chin sutured (the others were a guy who hit something and it looked like he tried to rip off his toe, and a girl that was a little scraped up – hard to get excited about stuff after you have seen what we have seen here). If it's not one trauma it is another. There is also a baby that is going to be born soon, which would be good after our start today.

But first, Bill and I walked Anne Rose to her plastic shelter tonight and walked among the city over there. There are ingenious shelter designs to say the least, but to walk in community with these people that have no house, very little to live on, and even less possessions was rather moving. I am sure it has its own rules and culture of walking around the edges of tents, and looking in, but I think because we are Americans, they have grace with us. The colors, even at 11pm in moonlight, cast shades of hope that define what it is like here. Of course there is misery, and naturally there is fear in not knowing how they will feed their children the next day. But only in Haiti have I seen over and over the resiliency that is endemic. Anyway, we were lost, although we knew where we had to go, and it was enjoyable to walk around, say, "Salu!" and "Bon Soir" to people we pass. It was good to be in the presence of those we serve, in their real life, in their world.

I love this place. I love these people. And the tent city is constantly changing with the addition of more each day.

## Back to the clinic

It apparently has been discovered that we have "late hours." Bill, Doug Pogue, Mary Beth and I go over to check on our infirm patients. Tonight we were called for the accident and also for the baby to come, but the place was filled with people. I think mostly a social scene, but all the same, it was crowded.

When I went down stairs this morning there were the contingent of our Navy doc and corpsmen. It was good to see them so early, and so we got off to a quick start. There was a woman having a breach baby, and the Navy doc was handling that, but they could not get the baby around. Bill had me find the cords, etc, for the cauterizing unit, which meant we might have to do and emergency C-section.

I had some running around to do get things ready in my hot pants (it was time to wash the other shorts again), and as I passed the sergeant of the Marines, who looks like he chews up marbles in the morning but is really nice and down to earth, I told him, "For the record, these shorts are not mine," and he came unglued. But then the

Navy doc, who loves the Haitians, had tears in her eyes as she was telling us the baby quit kicking and she couldn't hear the heartbeat anymore. I felt badly for her.

They did take her over to the heliport on the beach to ship her out along with a woman who had a nasty tibia/fibula fracture that has been that way since the earthquake. Doug went with them, and we never saw him again, figuring he went to the ship with them or something cool. When he did show up, his face was cooked. Turns out he was at the helipad for about 5 hours while they waited for a chopper to come get them. The Navy Doc was not happy, he said, and I appreciate that about her. She is totally for our patients. She told Bill today that she was glad he was there, and that made him feel great.

We had 2 patients that had a stroke today, too. One was an 85-year-old lady who we could do nothing for and sent her home with medicines after explaining the facts to her daughter. The other was a woman who was 50. She had hypertension (I took it at 160/110) and her entire left side was gone. Of course Bill pegged it quickly, but he is used to seeing it in the ER of IU Hospital.

Her sister was with her. There was only the sound of the air conditioner going, on 'fan' because the Haitians get cold. All the windows have been sealed with Plexiglas so that it is somewhat clean in there (our OR). The light cast a cheery yellow hue off the light-yellow walls, but it was not cheery in the least. Bill was great telling her about it. He is straight forward, but gentle and is so compassionate. The body language of the woman's sister, as it sunk in that this could be fatal, and we could do nothing even if it were in the US, told what was going through her soul.

As her legs quaked, we had her come and sit on the exam table between Bill and me, with Doug Pogue right in front of her. She stifled a sob and cried a little. As Bill tenderly prayed, I had to make myself cold to get through it without breaking down myself. Then her son came in, and he speaks amazing English. Bill explained it to him, and it was interesting to see the processing of it all, but so sad, and we all mourn for them. I know they are scared, and don't know what to do. Bill kept telling them how sorry he was for them, and I think they get that we really do care for them. We got her a bed on the other side by my office, and the 3 of us went over several times to make sure they were ok.

When I went back over tonight, I saw them and checked on her, and asked if there was anything we could do. While I was there, Manfred grabbed me and said something, and the son of the woman with a stroke came over and translated for me. Apparently his urine bag was full, and man, was it ever. You should have seen the look of contentment as I drained it.

Also found out that my assistant Ta has Sickle Cell anemia, and Ti Douglas has hemoglobin of 4. She is bringing him into the clinic to check, but it sounds like he could have it too. We had a wonderful talk today and I asked how she was, and all she wanted to talk about was her son. She is so good to me when we are working.

I sutured a guy who had a machete wound today. It sounds really wild, but it was his finger and I put in 3 sutures. Then came the story was it was really a stick. I told him to use the machete story, it sounds more macho.

I have a sinus infection and Doug P. and Bill have something going on too, but today my voice became deeper. I heard one of the Haitian staff say that I sounded like a man finally, joking to the others. Then someone else said, "Be careful, he speaks Creole!" (Which I don't, but understand a little more than I speak) and I turned around and winked and they all just died laughing. For those who know me, picture me with a voice an octave deeper wearing hot pants, walking around the clinic with stone white legs.

It is 1030 and off to check on Bill. I think he will spend the night over there to keep an eye on patients. Keep sending me emails . . . I love to, need to, wind down to them.

-   Doug

It is 12am, and I just returned from clinic. There is another baby on the way. Once again I was told to push on her stomach, as she was not helping any longer, but things were a ways off yet. As she was having a contraction, Bill noticed her water hadn't broken. He waited and then broke it at the exact moment she was pushing down even though she had not been pushing for the last hour or so.

It was shower city. Anne Rose and another Haitian nurse burst out laughing as Bill looked over his glasses at us. We laughed for a good few moments, and for those who do this for a living, I know this is probably not uncommon, but for the American Doc to have it done to him is somehow infinitely amusing to the others in the room.

She was not progressing and I was trying to take her BP, when she started to jerk around a bit . . . and then she erupted in projectile vomit. It was an awesome display, and the volume, the distance and the endurance of it all mesmerized me. It takes someone with semi-pro experience in this area to appreciate it, but it was a world-class effort. Thankfully she was moving away from me at the time. When I asked her how she was afterward, she quietly said, thru a vomit dripping mouth, in sing-song, "Pa pi mal," not too bad.

# Okay, a Little

**E**ntry #14 – January 29, 2010

Oui!! Merci Doctor, Merci Doctor," Avril said with a huge smile and her eyes bright. I had jumped on to the back of the Lifeline pickup truck and leaned in to ask if she was "Ca Va?" (Okay?). She was being transported to one of the US Navy ships, finally, and I was so happy for her. We were all ecstatic for her. We have had an amazing day in clinic and life today.

Public Service Announcement . . . Our relief group of Dave Pound, Chris Hartman, Patsy Phillips, Chrissa Belcher, and Jane Harris all made it. They wanted St Francis Hospital, the H.E.A.LT.H. Team, IG and H, Chapel Rock Christian Church, and their families to know they are well and excited to get going (I should be charging for all of these plugs). Now, back the events of the day.

One of our first patients was the 16-year-old girl I had written about early with the foot that was gangrenous and needed amputation. If you remember, we sent her to MSF (the French initials for Doctors Without Borders). I didn't recognize her at first. She was healthy and quite tall. When we unwrapped her leg, the amputation was amazingly good. She wanted crutches and basically a place to stay, so we let her stay out in the church part of the clinic. She was also a bit feisty, as she was demanding, but we liked to see her that way after we were not sure she was going to survive.

It was so bizarre today. A Navy Orthopedic Surgeon came in with a couple of other docs and corpsmen, and the place kind of went nutso. There were patients everywhere, Navy personnel all over the place, Bill was trying to point out who needed to be transported to ship, and I was trying to keep the Navy corpsmen supplied along with Doug P and Mary Beth.

The bench outside The OR was filled with "well baby checks," and the Haitian staff were seeing people and the church area was full, and corpsmen were out there, and NCIS wanted to talk to me because they couldn't find Bill, and it was crazy. But it was so fun, exciting, fluid, loud, anarchy . . . we just love it like that. People are still bringing in all kinds of injuries from the countryside. Another really bad fracture came in, and several other injuries. But the cool thing is the Navy transported the Paraplegic, the little girl with the hemoglobin of 4.4, several really bad fractures and the bad pelvis fracture that we had been trying to get on a ship. They took 9 of our worst patients today.

One of those they took was our sweet Anne Rose. The Navy orthopod knew she was important to us so he said he would give her the VIP treatment. These guys are the best. She was a little nervous, but was pleased to get her leg better as well.

Before things started cranking up this morning, I walked thru to make sure everyone was doing ok on the "ward." One of the paraplegics, when I asked him how he was, said he was, "okay, a little." I grabbed a translator to find out what that meant, culturally.

Sometimes what seems like a simple answer to a simple question is much more complex, and I sensed that this was one of those times.

What it meant was he was wondering what was going to happen with him. I realized that we had not said a thing to them other than we were trying to get them care someplace, which made no sense to them. He was totally respectful in his request, and that made me a little sick that I had been so obtuse to not keep him informed of what was happening.

I bent down beside him and explained that we were trying, the US Navy was trying and a group in the US was trying to get them somewhere where they could heal and learn to take care of themselves. I went on to remind him that I was here every morning, throughout the day, and at night to check on him to make sure he was ok and was wanting for nothing. I could tell the words I chose were being translated directly and I had embarrassed him.

He knew that I was only interested in what was the best for him, that we were not just let him go just anywhere, and we were trying to get him the best place possible. I also told him that many, many people in the US were praying for him and the others. And I begged his forgiveness for not keeping him up to date on what was happening, but I didn't even know all that was in the works to get him help.

He put his hand on mine and said, "Thank you," in the most humble manner I had ever heard. I told him my favorite part of the day was to come over to talk and pray with him and the others, and I would not let anything happen that was not in his best interest. He is not alone in this, I am in it with him, and so are Dr. Bill, Doug, and Mary Beth. Then I asked if he understood how much we cared for him? He did. I asked if he knew how much more God loved him than we ever could. And he nodded his head vigorously with a smile. I went around the corner and once again wept.

The lady with the stroke looked lots better today. Her son, who speaks great English, asked if she could stay again tonight. I asked him why, and he said he didn't know what he would do if . . . . I talked it over with Doug, and he asked Bill's opinion, and we agreed it would be fine. They are scared, and her blood pressure is coming down since we have been mashing up her pill and with a rolled up paper kind of funneling it under her tongue.

There was another really strong aftershock today that felt like we had been dumped off a table. It was big, and the Haitians went scurrying around trying to get outside. We were in clinic and didn't move, but everyone that could ran. The Haitian staff wouldn't look at me as they came back in.

Not long after that, a missionary at an orphanage came in with one of their charges. When the aftershock hit, he jumped up so fast he hit his head on the concrete stairs above him and made a 2.5-inch gash in his head. I sewed it up for him. He was a little embarrassed about it, and I gave him a hard time.

At the same time Doug brought in a patient that shuffled in slowly and as he was examining her, thought she had a pelvic fracture.

On top of that she had leaves stuffed in her underwear. Doug asked what that was about, and I told him she had been to the "Leaf Doctor," a Voodoo witch doctor. Often their remedies are right on, but not this one. We had her hang on until tonight, and Bill examined her and concurred with Doug. I asked Ben to ask her if she fell and the wall fell on top of her, or did the wall fall and hitting her. Although I could not understand it, I could see her hand movements showing how she was trying to run and the floors and the walls were going back and forth, and she tried to avoid one wall but was thrown into another, etc. You could feel the terror as she told the story.

Finally, the medical team I talked about before came in tonight. That means Bill and I get to start home on Saturday. We want to transition with the new team tomorrow, and then start on our way home. It was great to see those I love and have traveled with many times to Haiti. Dave, one of my closest friends and a doctor, has saved my life twice, now.

Patsy, Chrissa, and Jane are like my sisters, and Patsy and Chrissa hugged me like I have needed for a week. Chris is a great guy and I really like his sense of humor. He is an ER guy at St Francis. He has been here once with us, and he has one of those personalities that connects with mine immediately (and he is even normal). He and Bill are two peas in a pod, and all is well in the emergency area. I almost wept when Dave and Chris came in the door at the OR in the clinic tonight. Man it was good to see them.

Also, I have been in contact with John Walker, M.D. from Mount Pleasant Christian Church. They are on the ground and working in Port au Prince. Tammy, I ran into Franz today and I will meet with him today.

Tonight as I walked over from the clinic, before the team arrived, I strolled through the tent city and just tried to enjoy the ambiance of the place I watched grow and will be leaving soon. There was a church service going on, like it does every night, and the sounds of church, the glows of fires and coals burning in and around the tarps of every color, gave a light of warmth and love that beckons me to stay a little longer. People from everywhere call me by name (Dr Doug), and the children come out to hold my hand as I walk. It is a mystical, wonderful stroll, and I will miss these people I love so much.

More tomorrow,
Doug

## Uncleanliness

H ey,

From the airport in Port au Prince, Haiti, that looks nothing like the airport of old. The US has control of it. There is no immigration, and no customs, no exit stamp on my passport, not much of anything. We are going in through the exit, as the old ticketing area is ruined.

I sit in a hallway that leads to a little area that has a door that leads to the tarmac. The only sound is quiet talk and the roar of a distant jet warming its turbines. There is a group of trauma surgeons from LA and their support. They are really nice people and get what this is about (not expecting to having anything up and running, making do with what is around you, treating patients as people and loving on them).

They have been talking with us and taping our stories. There are about 758,000 flies landing all over you when you stop moving for a minute. I have given up trying to keep them off of me. A federal agent wearing dark blue with a side arm strapped to his side comes by and tells me that the floor I am sitting on is really filthy. I thank him and continue typing, remembering what I have sat in, kneeled in, held, had splashed on me, and seen the last two weeks. I could eat off of this floor. I love this place.

After our relief team from St Francis arrived Thursday night, we sat up on the roof for a couple of hours and updated, and unloaded on them. This was purposeful on their part to air us out a little and to get some perspective of what to expect. I appreciate them giving us a chance to vent and get "it" out of us. This is a group we have traveled with for many years and we are like family.

Friday, we were up early and at it, and it was good to have the St Francis team working with us. To be honest, I was not exactly chomping at the bit, because they were here. I wanted to watch them work and I needed to get a grip on things. I was pushing it, physically. I had five dental patients but just could not do it anymore. The Haitian dentist is starting up on Monday, and none of these cases were tragic.

The Navy was back in full swing and as Bill did his thing, I talked to the US Public Health about what we saw as coming needs, and I think they talked to Bill to get the real story. Latrines, inoculations (we have heard there is a measles and tetanus outbreak in Leogane and PaP), basic hygiene supplies, and everything else a person might need.

I cannot tell you how much less than nothing these people have. The girl with the amputation has not changed her clothes in 19 days. She has no clothes other than what she is wearing, although we are working on it. It is nice to see her act like any other 16-year-old, and the amputation is down the list of her needs at this time. She is a feisty demanding teenager, and I think she will do fine because of the attitude.

Ta showed up with her two kids and I got to hold Ti Doug (as in "Petit" or Little Doug). I can already tell he is a genius, really handsome, and will undoubtedly grow up to be a bruiser, like his namesake. Ti Ta (or "Douglina!" Ta says exasperated to me when she is referring her daughter as she runs names together so fast) had a fever and was vomiting. Chrissa looked at her and gave her some medication. Ti Doug, had a hemoglobin of 9, so he is shaping up. We prayed with her and her family, and it was nice to see such a sweet family unit. Ta was quite thrilled to show him off, but not nearly as much as I was to see, hold, and pray for him. It is one of my prized relationships here.

People are coming in from the countryside now. There was a bad tib/fib fracture, a kid with a large laceration on his head, and a little boy that had a femur fracture. This is how it will be for the foreseeable future. At the same time, clinic is becoming a little more normal, which is a good thing. Those in the outlying areas will start to make their way in to the clinic. Those who are the poorest of the most impoverished country in the western hemisphere; who are always forgotten; who are neglected; who are always last, will make their way to the clinic.

**The Quest**

Moses told me he knew where she was. We walked through town in the blazing heat, in, out and around the "new" houses that are springing up in the street. Her name is Jeseline, and my family has supported her for years. I had not seen or heard of her until a little while ago (I have no concept of what day it is). She was living in a rickety place before, but I had been quite worried about her. I had not seen her and everyone I asked said they had not seen her, which is like saying she was dead.

Except for Moses, who said singsong, "OOOH, she is alright, and I know where she is living." Finally, I was able to find time to search her out. As we walked around one street tent, Moses stopped and I ran right into him. He was talking to a woman and as I came around him she glanced at me, and we recognized each other at the same moment. She had a huge grin on her face, and came over and kissed me. She then called out "Jeseline!" and this face looked up from a group sitting on the ground and she broke into a smile, came running over to me as well, and then her sister who always accompanies her came right after her, and it was a cute little reunion. Their house had partially collapsed, and they were too scared to go in and get much of their belongings from it.

I started that way to pull some stuff out and they all shrieked in horror. Moses said, calmly, quietly, "They think it would not be a good idea for you to go in there." I told him I got that part, and he smiled and slapped me on the back. I gave them money, and we prayed together. I had no idea how much that had been weighing on me, but my step was a little lighter as that burden was eased.

Last night, I had devotions, and they were on the roof. I had written a sermon (I usually preach on Tuesday night) intending to talk about the Christmas story and how the angels appeared to shepherds by night; how He was born in a stable, and how David, who was of his lineage was a shepherd (thanks to Seth and Shan). And yes, those shepherds were scared to death when the Angels appeared. I would be scared to death too if an Angel were to appear to me in a Godly brilliance.

Being a shepherd defined lowliness in the first century. It was a profession that was looked down upon. Jesus had come from line of almost the worst profession one could have, and was born into a place of filth and uncleanliness. Uncleanliness was a big deal in the first century Jewish tradition, and the unclean were shunned like the impoverished are today. He was born of poverty to be with the impoverished, to love those who no one else loved.

Then I was going to end it with the second verse of my new favorite Christmas Carol that my daughter, Brittany, turned me onto, "Oh Holy Night," that says: "Truly he taught us to love one another, his law is love and his gospel is peace. Chains shall he break for the slave is our brother, and in his name all oppression shall cease."

Tying all of this together, I was going to talk about how we had served, loved, prayed, and lived along side of the oppressed, the unloved, the unwanted, the filthy, for the last two weeks and were honored to be considered their brothers. Jesus came to earth for those who are exactly in their position, their condition. He came to alleviate their distress, their oppression, their poverty, their slavery . . . often times those who are literally enslaved, but also like all of us, enslaved to our sins. He came to break those chains that hold them, hold us back from experiencing Him and a true love that is unmistakable, the best kind of love that never fails, that is always looking for us if we just accept it. Looking over this, I wish I had gone with it.

But there had been several requests to hear my story. After consulting with Dave about the wisdom of the same story for the umpteenth time (which he thought a great idea). I went with it. So for those who are sick of hearing about it, skip down, now.

I was physically broken, like the Haitians say Haiti is now, finished, like they speak of their nation. But 13 years, 5 months and 14 days ago the phone rang and the voice said, "Doug, this is Liz at Transplant (Indiana University Medical Center) . . . it is time." It is time.

I had been sick for 8 years with a progressive, incurable liver disease called Primary Sclerosing Cholangitis. Two famous people who had it were Walter Payton, NFL Hall of Fame and arguably the best running back in history, and I understand the son of Robert Redford. Obviously, it strikes really athletic, handsome men.

Of course, this meant someone had died so I could live. Somewhere, a husband or wife, father or mother, daughter or son had gone off to work, to school, to play, to shop, to visit a friend, and their family never saw their loved one alive again. Then, in the most tragic moment of their lives, a moment I pray I will never experience, a family decided that they loved me enough, without knowing me, to donate organs so their loved one's life would not be the end, but would go on living in me.

Ever since we knew the diagnosis and its implications, and since my transplant, we have prayed for that family, knowing the pain they would endure every day for the rest of their lives. I pray that somehow God will assuage their anguish, will comfort them in this gift they have given me, us, and our family.

Briefly that was, this is my story. And it is the best thing that has ever happened to me. I am a better husband, father, son, brother, cousin, friend, boss, and lover of God than I think I would have ever been without being close to death, without needing such a sacrifice.

My donor was the second person to die for me. You see some 2000 years ago another man died so I might live in Eternity. I needed a transplant of my soul and He willing died so I could receive it, the kind of transplant anyone can have.

Anyway, I wanted to relate that life is full of second chances, whether it is literally a second chance, like me, or by rebuilding a house, a community, and nation like Haiti. All of the second chances in life are through love, and loving one another is all we really do that really matters. It wasn't the setting bones, the caring for bed sores, the emptying of urine, the sewing up, taking blood pressures, holding people limbs in place while Bill pulled and manipulated the bones back into position, or the antibiotics, or one Tylenol every eight hours we would give a kid who had his face gouged, and an eye nearly ripped out for pain relief because we were nearly out.

No, it was when we were down on our knees beside those that are oppressed, those who are enslaved to poverty, pain, helplessness and fear and those no one else wanted, and for whom no one else cared. It was lying beside the paraplegic on their level, or more precisely them beside me on my level. It was Bill holding the hand of the sister of the stroke victim telling her how sorry he was for both of them, and praying for her so tenderly. It was the exposed face of a little boy ripped open by a piece of random concrete falling onto him during a random earthquake, and Bill turning away to gather himself, as I tried not to soil the sterile area of work with my tears. It was looking at a mother's face as it is explained to her that her daughter might die if we cut off her leg, may die during us cutting off her leg and certainly would die if we did not cut off her leg, and without hesitation telling Bill it was in God's hands and she trusted his judgment.

It was the last thing I did in the clinic after devotions. I went over to say goodbye to the paraplegics, to tell them I was leaving, but Doug Pogue, Mary Beth, Patsy, Chrissa, and Jane would take good care of them. It was trying to pull myself together to make it through a prayer for them, but they were really ministering to me with strength I will never possess. My asking how they are and their respond with "Ca va," and "Pa pi mal." Not too bad. And then it was walking off just far enough so that Patsy could hold me while I sobbed into her, because the only way I will ever see those 2 men alive again is if God intervenes, and they both know it, you can see it in their eyes. They have taught me so much, so many things about living with dignity in an undignified manner with no privacy, open to flies and heat and cold nights, and never once complaining. And I sobbed some more, trying to catch my breath. Love and being loved repairs so much, fixes the unfixable.

# Summary

T hese two weeks have been the most intense mission time I have ever experienced. I don't know why it was Bill and I that got in to Haiti when so many others were trying. I do know it was not by accident.

Here is the deal. We were a good fit with each other, and I cannot imagine doing this with anyone else. Bill is incredibly gifted, brilliant, and has the biggest heart I have ever seen. We worked as hard and as long as humanly possible. I don't know if we saved anyone's life, but I know people would have died had we not been here. More than that, we tried to be obedient, sought, begged for God's mercy on us in the treatment, care and love of every person we saw. We were as obedient to God's Word as we could be, and prayed with every, and I mean every patient we saw. I hope we honored Him in all of this.

I learned it is not what you need, but what you have that counts. Not how many supplies, but what you can do with them, and trust God to give you enough (took me awhile to get that one). Also to use what is around you, whether cardboard boxes, or palm bark, string or duct tape, and prayer seems to mend things that we cannot. When our supplies were just a tiny pile, we were blessed with much more from Doctors Without Borders, other teams leaving (thank you La-Porte), and the Navy and Marines. I knew this, but the lesson was drilled into me that it matters to spend time with people.

Time is the one thing we were in the shortest supply of when so many were injured. But we promised we would see every patient that was there, and it may have taken 18 hours, but they were seen, and the power of following through pays off every time. I learned that one could be taught tenderness by a child exercising the leg of a paralyzed mother. A lesson in patience from people who wait 5 days to be seen and are still grateful for everything you do for them and give them.

I found out we have a really incredible Armed Forces. They care about the people of Haiti, which by extension means all of us care about Haiti. I was impressed with and touched by the compassion they treated our patients and friends with, and they transported some 40 or 50 patients to the ships for care that we could not possibly provide.

I confess to being a little ashamed of myself. This story is about the Haitian people, but it has turned out to be rather self-centered. It is written through my eyes, so that you might experience what I was—we were doing. I hope I have conveyed the strength, resilience and courage, and work ethic of these people, because they are amazing. Bill and I both love these people and this country. I have learned an incredible amount in short time, and am grateful for every minute, even the tough and terrible minutes I still cannot talk about.

What I will remember, always, is the Marines coming in and saying, "We're looking for two docs from Indiana."

# Eiplogue

About a week ago, I returned from Grand Goave, Haiti. Bill, I, and several other medical types including my wife Debbie, joined a construction team to work there. Are things different? Certainly. The clinic is open, and fairly back to normal. I was in my dental suite giving beautiful women their smiles back by fixing holes in front teeth. But the world does not live in the clinic, in my suite. It lives in the town, in the tents that everyone seems to have. There is a new timeline. B.E. and A.E. Before Earthquake, After Earthquake. Simple as that, and as complicated as that. It is hard to make accurate generalizations from just a week, mostly in a clinic, so I won't. But I will write about what I saw.

AnneRose is back in Grand Goave after time on the ship, and several months of therapy on the Dominican Republic border. Her knee is better but has limited movement. Her smile and her heart are as beautiful and healthy as ever—her defining characteristic. She is living in a tent behind the clinic with her two sisters.

The Tent City has been transferred there, and people now live in these huge, blue tents for two families courtesy of Samaritan's Purse. They have a few possessions and two beds—or more appropriately, a few layers of cardboard, on wood, on top of blocks. It is hard and uncomfortable, and I don't know how she can lay there for any more than a few minutes.

When we went in to see her place one afternoon, it was well over 130 degrees, and I had trouble breathing the air was so hot. Yet, this is Haiti. What people endure, what they live every day, without complaining, is beyond my imagination.

Don't worry for AnneRose, a few people on the team went in to purchase her a new home to be built sometime in the reasonable future. She was rather excited, as in, she wept. She kissed people and hugged and kissed some more and she was overjoyed. She deserves it.

But what of all the other families in the Tent City, in Grand Goave, in Haiti, what becomes of them? Because we know her, because it is outrageous for her to live there when it can be changed, she's the one who gets help? Why am I not outraged enough to help everyone else? My heart struggles, and I try to make sense of it all, but it is complicated, and I am not smart enough to do the math of it all. I am still learning and sorting through what I can do, and what my heart wants to do, and what I think Jesus calls me to do.

The paraplegics (those whom I love and cared for) are in Port au Prince at a place there that has been established for them. I was hoping to see them, but that was not to be.

Bill stuck his head in my dental office one morning and said, "You have to see this." When I went out, it was one of the boys who had his legs crushed. Frankly, and I am ashamed to write this, I did not spend much time thinking about after we prayed, because I knew he would die of kidney failure in a few weeks. At the time, there were too many more to see, to worry about, and to keep praying over, and I had to let him go. But there he was smiling at us, and I could not believe my eyes. His legs were like sticks but he was alive (even as I write I am smiling). His brother was with him, the one I wrote of with the fractured humerus and so many slings. They were both glad to see Bill and me, but not nearly as much as we were to see them. Sarah, a new athletic trainer graduate, worked with those two and wrote last Monday that he was walking on his own. God is so good.

I have several other stories of patients who didn't know they were dead yet, and I did not write of in January, who showed up walking, too. It was so amazing to see it all. All those I thought would be dead, that though the odds were against them, they live, and are doing well, and remembered Bill and me.

The man I wrote of who had the bladder the size of a rump roast that Bill had to do a suprapubic tap into his bladder, came to see us. He went on ship to have a treatment for his prostate and was in to see us because he was still leaking from his tap site. But he was glad to see us, and we talked and sewed him tight. Now he no longer leaks. Another satisfied customer.

The woman who had the serious stroke that Bill so tenderly explained to her sister the circumstances of her condition and she about collapsed, we heard had died. This is life, and this is death in Haiti.

Everyone seems to be living in tents, even if their houses aren't too badly damaged. There are still a few aftershocks, nothing remotely like we experienced when we were there, but enough that people are still too scared to sleep in their homes... and the rainy season just started with hurricane season upon them.

God, please have mercy on these brave, beautiful and incredible people. They have suffered so much already. I love them, Lord, and I am one of them. I am Haitian.

- Doug

# Acknowledgements

I would like to thank Joyce Long for making me do this, and the hours and hours she spent editing my words and thoughts. I could not have done this without her, would not have even thought to do it without her, and I appreciate her gobs. She inspired me to continue, and kept telling how much others would like to read what we experienced as we worked alongside the Haitian people.

I would also like to thank Luke Webb, who edited and corrected when Joyce and I could no longer see straight. He was particularly helpful in keeping me on target with verb tense and with my lack of writing skills in general. He also is the best son-in-law a man could have. Thank you to Brittany and Luke as you teach me every day about what it is to follow Christ, but also the encouraging me to travel, especially this time, knowing I had to go. I am so proud of you, everything you do. I love you for who you are and cannot wait to see what God has in store for your future.

I could not do any of this without the blessing and love of a wonderful and perfect wife who knows my heart and allows me to go, by encouraging me to serve Him—even when it means extended periods away from her (or maybe that is why???). Thank you!

Thanks to Bill for all he taught me. For his wisdom and words which I borrowed generously in this writing.

When I wrote "we" about 90% of the time it was "he" as in Bill, but "we" as in I was present.

I would like to thank Bob Bashum of Outback Steakhouse and Walkabout Air for our spectacular rides in and out.

Lifeline Christian Mission (Lifeline.org) who did everything for us, from food to translators to cleaning up after us, to having the clinic we worked from. To Gretchen for her tireless work and love, and Bob for getting the place back together... this is going to be a long process.

The Center For Global Impact (centerforglobalimpact.org) who gave me money for medicine, emergencies, to help people who needed immediate help, and for the tap tap ride to Grand Goave - CGI is an amazing mission.

Indian Creek Christian Church provided incredible prayer, love and guidance throughout my time in Haiti and in my life. I belong to a church that lives the first century church model.

I need to thank the staff at my office whose work and dedication allow me to travel and live my dream without losing the quality of care of serving our patients. So thank you Sherri, Michele, Patty, Kim, Cathy, Jenni, Carrisa, Nanette, Shane, and Ann (and anyone else that may have subbed) for all you do and for the goodies you send along with supplies.

To my patients, thank you. You are the ones that support such trips. Without you coming to our office, I could never afford to go because actually you are the ones supporting me. Thank you again and again.

Finally, to my God. For without Him I am nothing.

- Doug

Breinigsville, PA USA
15 February 2011
255586BV00002B/1/P